Toll Free

Scriptural Insight, Inspiration and Devotionals for Every Day

Pearl C. White

HCM PUBLISHING
Lancaster, Texas

HCM PUBLISHING
Lancaster, Texas

Copyright pending 2012 by Pearl C. White

All rights reserved. No part of this book may be used or reproduced in any manner whatsoever without written permission except in case of brief quotations.

All quotations and references to Scripture, unless otherwise indicated, have been taken from the King James Version of the Bible.

Toll Free *Scriptural Insights, Inspiration and Devotionals for Every Day* is Published by HCM Publishing

Toll Free *Scriptural Insights, Inspiration and Devotionals for Every Day Printed in the United States of America. The views expressed are the author's only. For information address inquiries to HCM Publishing, P.O. Box 36, Lancaster, TX 75146*

Cover design by White's Printing and Graphic Design

First Edition

ISBN-10:0975334255
ISBN-13:978-0-9753342-5-6

This book is dedicated to the memory of my mother

Mrs. Mattie L. T. Daniels

And My Grandchildren
Thomas
Jasmin
Grant
Gabrielle
Alyssa
Victorya

To mother…thank you for my earliest memories of courage and incredible strength in living color. Looking back to my childhood years, I recall the lessons you taught me as you faced times of hopelessness, disappointments and the many sacrifices of widowhood with a two year old little girl. These lessons were not taught to me with textbooks, pencils or paper. Only the recollections of your constant reminders and your unwavering faith that "we'll make it, with God's help."

Without your motherly love and influence, Toll Free would remain unorganized notes, unwritten thoughts and inspirational gleanings from God. Thank you Madear.

Contents

Foreword	vi
Preface	viii
Acknowledgements	x
Introduction	xii
Chapter One *Unlimited Minutes*	1
Chapter Two *Have Faith in God*	17
Chapter Three *Trusting God Through the Struggle*	33
Chapter Four *Go and Tell the Good News!*	45
Chapter Five *Accept What He Has to Offer*	51

Chapter Six *He Offers World Wide Coverage*	57
Chapter Seven *It's Your Choice*	63
Chapter Eight *The Unlimited Power of God*	72
Chapter Nine *Service Agreements*	79
Chapter Ten *Your Faithfulness Commends You to God*	89
Chapter Eleven *Rid Yourself of the Negative and Accept God's Love*	102
Chapter Twelve *Eternity is For Everyone*	117
Chapter Thirteen *Discipleship*	135
Affirmations From A-Z	153

Foreword

The 21st century finds the world in a state of rapid change. With the latest technological advancement business meetings are held in various states or even countries via Skype, or grandmothers sing lullabies to their grandchildren over webcams. We welcome all positive change; however, we must remember to take time to communicate with our Loving Father. Philippians 4:8 admonishes us to keep aground by meditating on whatever is pure, right, holy, friendly and proper. The believer must continually think on things wholesome and worthy of praise.

District Missionary Pearl C. White is a leader in the Church of God in Christ and sees a need for constancy in spiritual discipline. She offers to the world a book propagating these virtues. *"Toll Free: Insights, Inspiration and Devotions for Every Day,"* fuses stories such as *The Wise Gladly Accept Wisdom, First Things First, and Is My Life A Clear Reproduction of Christ?* with Scripture to allow reflection on their faith, relationships, salvation and helps individuals as they journey through life. With the Scripture printed with each story *Toll Free* is an excellent tool for both private devotions and sharing in Bible Study groups.

With so much to distract us from the faith, our libraries should have easy-to-read books such as *Toll Free* which offers a wealth of solace and comfort. I commend Mother White for bringing this fine literary work into being.

Mrs. Willie Mae Rivers
Sixth International Supervisor, Department of Women
Church of God in Christ, Inc.
October 2011

Preface

Toll Free contains insights on Scripture texts which give some elements of truth to the selected text and day to day life experiences. The illustrations are easily understood by *all ages and* individuals in all walks of life. They are accompanied by Scriptures that are discussed using the King James Version of the Bible unless otherwise noted. The book also contains some personal testimonies of the author.

The focal point of *Toll Free* points the reader through the Word of God to the ease, uncomplicated and unlimited access to develop a one-to-one relationship with the Savior. It is hoped that the reader will realize that he is afforded immediate personal contact with Christ for salvation, guidance and help in the time of need. I Peter 3:18 "For Christ also died for sins once for all, the just for the unjust, in order that He might bring us to God…" The book title reminds the reader of the pre-arranged plan so that no expense is involved, "no middle man," no equipment breakdowns, no calls placed on hold and *Toll Free* shows the reader that God is truly available. *"And it shall be that everyone who calls on the name of the Lord shall be saved."* Acts 2:21 NASV

Toll Free is written to be used as a source of inspiration, encouragement, and personal or group devotional studies. It also offers ideas for sermon preparation and messages helps.

Toll Free will strengthen and renew the reader's Christian walk and offers the unbeliever hope in the ever present and all powerful love of the, "only wise God our Savior" in all the universe.

Acknowledgements

I am indebted to every individual who has been a consistent source of encouragement in this effort. They have provided invaluable assistance in the completion of *TOLL FREE*.

A special word of thanks is given to Bishop Roy L.H. Winbush, Jurisdictional Prelate, Louisiana First Jurisdiction as well as the Department of Women's Supervisor Vanessa Winbush Gatlin. My sincere appreciation to Rev. E. Edward Jones for sharing your wisdom and kind words of encouragement. Very special thanks to my friend Mrs. Gloria Millender for her kindness and assistance.

Glenda Williams Goodson and I prayed together and she generously shared her professional expertise in the book's evolution to the finished product.

I deeply appreciate Mrs. Willie Mae Rivers, the International Supervisor of the Department of Women of the Churches of God in Christ, for taking time from her busy schedule to write the Foreword.

To my husband Walter along with our children Tania White Jackson, MD and her husband Gary, Kristi, Elder Walter N. White, Jr., his wife Shronda and my friend Beverly, thank you for providing me with the gifts of your enduring patience, generosity, and technical support. Your prayers helped me to stick to the integrity of the message revealed to my heart. Without your loving efforts it would not have been possible to complete this book.

Introduction

During the latter 1960s, before it was considered popular to publicly wear wigs as an accessory, I was forced to use a hair piece. It was necessary to cover missing patches of hair as a result of the tremendous stress I was experiencing. At that time we lived in the vicinity of the Shreveport Regional Airport and our pastor was Bishop J.W. White, formerly the Prelate of Western Louisiana Jurisdiction presently, First Jurisdiction of Louisiana. Bishop White often entertained guest speakers and if they stayed overnight or had a flight out of the city, at his request we opened our home to them and served as their hosts until to their departure from the city.

Elder John Lawrence was one such guest and as he was leaving for the airport he left a pink track with us to read entitled *"What Must I Do To Be Saved?"* We accepted it and thanked him. Upon our return home I safely stored the tract on the bookshelf out of sight where it remained for years.

One day while dusting I saw a portion of the pink leaflet sticking out of the bookshelf and quickly moved it back in place—out of sight—and I continued my chores. Several months passed after this incident once again I noticed the pink leaflet sticking out from the neat row of books in full view. I could not imagine why it was continuously reappearing. Two or three weeks later while walking through the living room I was astonished (and I might add somewhat leery) to find the "pink sheet" sticking out of the books on the shelf for the third time. It was at that moment I felt a strong urge to read it to see if there was a message to me. Sitting on the floor I began reading the "pink sheet" for the first time. I was in tears as I finished and under such conviction of the sin in my life that I gave my life to Christ and made a promise to Him. I promised Him if He would give me the promises found in the "pink sheet" that I would make copies and give them out wherever possible. He kept every promise. The stress left and my hair was restored.

I have made copies by the thousands, leaving them on trains, buses, airplanes, mailing them in monthly bills with my checks. I have given them to repairmen with a brief statement of purpose. I have even placed them in greeting cards, used them as house to house witnessing tools and for Bible Study during revivals. These are some of the ways of keeping my promise and to express my thanks to God for salvation. TOLL FREE is also a way for me to share God's plan of salvation with accompanying Scriptures to those persons who may not own a Bible.

The change in my life made by that little tract nicknamed by our children the "pink sheet," reinforced my faith in the vastness of the harvest that can be reaped when God's Word is sown. When planted in the hearts of men, women, and children, whether it is through a tract, a testimony, the preached Word or from a book of everyday life experiences that same change can be made in your life. Some are in the raw, some inconceivable and unbelievable as are many of the life challenges in TOLL FREE. The extremity of your situation whether on land, under the earth, beneath the ocean, or in the air, God's invitation remains, *"Come Unto Me"* from any point in the universe. Distance is not a problem, your call will be expected and accepted, it is TOLL FREE. *Romans 8:30-31; Psalm 139:8-12.*

Pearl Cooper White
Shreveport, Louisiana

CHAPTER ONE

Unlimited Minutes

Daniel Predicts the Increase of Knowledge

Facebook, YouTube, IPod, Twitter, MySpace, video posting, Google, Blackberry, texting, sexting, IPhone, Skyping—are all words that were nonexistent in technology just three or four years ago. Their coined usage today in high tech terminology is farfetched from the definitions found in today's general dictionary. In fact, most of these terms will not be in today's English dictionary. This rapid increase in knowledge was prophesied—thousands of years ago by the writer of the Book of Daniel in the Old Testament.

The words we've listed are a sampling of words relatively new in technology. In every area of science, industry, communication, transportation, fashion, musical expression and even in food service, there are word combinations unique to the industry. These newly coined terms are used to describe the concoctions, mixtures, and blends of food, breads, drinks, etc.

The increase in knowledge may also be viewed as "signs of the times." These signs tell us by this increase in knowledge through technology, we are closer to the occasion when Jesus will keep His promise of returning to earth for those who have prepared themselves through their righteous lifestyles, for His return.

> ### Daniel 12:4
> 4But thou, O Daniel, shut up the words, and seal the book, even to the time of the end: many shall run to and fro, and knowledge shall be increased.
>
> ### 1 Thessalonians 4:16-18
> 16For the Lord himself shall descend from heaven with a shout, with the voice of the archangel, and with the trump of God: and the dead in Christ shall rise first: 17Then we which are alive and remain shall be caught up together with them in the clouds, to meet the Lord in the air: and so shall we ever be with the Lord. 18Wherefore comfort one another with these words.

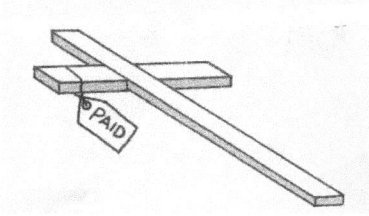

The "Wait" Time

In a number of procedures involving chemical or natural compound mixtures the desired results will not be realized until a certain time frame has elapsed. This time is period is known as the 'wait time", the "set time," or the "jell" period. These time periods may vary from process to process, but with all things in order the formations will slowly take place.

The writer of the Book of Acts shares the promise of Jesus to His disciples. Jesus commands them in His farewell address to remain and not to travel from the city but to look for the very special promise. A promise always refers to a future event. In this case they were to remain together and wait for the arrival of the Holy Spirit.

The only thing certain about the unheard of promise was that it would come, it would not disappoint them, but they would only realize the joy of receiving it if they obeyed His specific command to WAIT — wait until it appears, no given date and no estimated time. They were to be patient, faithful, calm, expectant and wait, because He that promised, will come.

Day one, the group felt He would probably come tomorrow or by the third day.

Day four came and left with some in the group beginning to wonder if they heard right. In fact, they may have reasoned, perhaps this time could be better spent. There were many personal things that were getting behind. After all they were losing money just being there day after day.

Day five, day six some of them had to persuade others to remain. In their conversation they urged their friends, "not to leave just yet, wait a little longer because Jesus had never failed to keep a promise to them. Remember his good friend, Lazarus? Even though he died, when Jesus made His arrival everything was wonderful."

Day seven, then *day eight* and nothing, only cramped quarters, hunger pangs, discomfort. But the singing, praying and Scriptures took on new meaning and the joy was unbelievable.

Day nine nothing changed except the joy of the Lord was even greater. The thoughts of home, the outside world and even family affairs were overshadowed by the presence of the Holy Spirit.

Then day number ten, the day of Pentecost and it happened! While it was not as they expected, this was nothing like they ever dreamed. It was Wonderful, Marvelous, Indescribable! The long wait was over, just as He promised. Yes, He kept His promise and the promise of the Father was given to all those who waited in faith.

There are areas in our lives that we are in need of a change that only God can make. We have His promises and can be assured when we remove our focus from the time factor and wait with patience for His timing of the One who controls our times—our past, present, and future. He will not neglect us. He will keep every promise.

The Ten Virgins

Prepared? From all appearances they had everything they needed, all the equipment, all the gear, their luggage was filled with the best attire and was ready at a moment's notice to slip into. As they lined up, they looked beautiful, all dressed in white, ready to march because the bridegroom was nigh. But one thing was missing: They looked the same, their singing was the same, they quoted the same Scriptures, they even prayed and joined in on the same days of fasting. But, five of them were not allowed to take the trip. They had one item missing, but no one knew because all the virgins looked alike although they were not all alike.

We can be faithful in the church, singing, carrying on the praise, participating in the drives, working the altar, have a powerful testimony, but one item is missing and no one knows it is absent. The ones who tried to get a light could only get black smoke and fumes because there was no oil *in the* wick.

It seems impossible that after all the planning, all the packing, and all the farewells they would not be going on that trip after all. They were rejected because of one little missing but essential requirement (without it, no one will see the Lord in peace.) They did not have any oil. Oil in the Scriptures is representative of the Holy Spirit. One may speak as though they have it, they may even preach and teach as though they have it. However, the time will come when imitations will no longer suffice because the day of reckoning will be upon us. Today you may be in the right place, at the right time but aware that you do not have all that you need to get you into the presence of the Father and the Son in peace.

The virgins may have allowed pride, a false sense of security; shame and fear of what others would think prevent them from asking for the missing oil. And when it was time to get in the line-up they could not see because of the black smoke and stinking fumes. They began to ask, beg, cry and plead for mercy from anyone to give them some oil. They even offered to pay any price, but their money could not buy it. It can only be acquired by repenting, believing and receiving the oil of the Holy Spirit.

Come to the Lord while it is called today. You have many yesterdays, only one today and tomorrow is not promised. It may be that you had some oil at one time and you realize it is out, or you may have never asked for it because it was not desired, but today you see that it is the Lord's plan for your life and there is no substitute. There are some lookalikes but this Oil cannot be reproduced.

> *Matthew 25:1-13*
> [1]*Then shall the kingdom of heaven be likened unto ten virgins, which took their lamps, and went forth to meet the bridegroom.* [2]*And five of them were wise, and five were foolish.* [3]*They that were foolish took their lamps, and took no oil with them:* [4]*But the wise took oil in their vessels with their lamps.* [5]*While the bridegroom tarried, they all slumbered and slept.* [6]*And at midnight there was a cry made, Behold, the bridegroom cometh; go ye out to meet him.* [7]*Then all those virgins arose, and trimmed their lamps.* [8]*And the foolish said unto the wise, Give us of your oil; for our lamps are gone out.* [9]*But the wise answered, saying, Not so; lest there be not enough for us and you: but go ye rather to them that sell, and buy for yourselves.* [10]*And while they went to buy, the bridegroom came; and they that were ready went in with him to the marriage: and the door was shut.* [11]*Afterward came also the other virgins, saying, Lord, Lord, open to us.* [12]*But he answered and said, Verily I say unto you, I know you not.* [13]*Watch therefore, for ye know neither the day nor the hour wherein the Son of man cometh.*

Three Little Ships and God's Providence

The Nina, *The* Pinta and *The* Santa Maria set sail out on the Pacific, the largest ocean on earth. The ships were loaded with provisions but the crew consisted mainly of passengers with little seafaring knowledge or equipment. There was no steam for speed and no oil for pressure. They depended primarily on the wind, the sails and the guidance of God.

The only source of energy to move them over the mighty ocean waters were neither by any earthly might, nor earthly power but by the Spirit of God. Hours, days and days of coasting, sometimes eastward, westward and sometimes being swept backward by fierce gusts of wind and rain. There were times they were almost motionless—just bobbing up and down. At other times they seemed to move uncontrollably in circles. Then without any warning the answer to their prayers was on the horizon, the sky was a clear blue, the winds blew softly and as if guided by some unseen nautical system all three ships followed a straight course toward the shores of the new land.

Life at times resembles the journey of the three ships out on the unchartered waters of a great ocean, without sufficient charts, compasses or telescopes to learn their physical bearings or gain some sense of directions in their trials.

Just as the occupants of those three little ships were people of great faith in God, believers in the Bible and in the power of prayer, we must not relinquish our trust in God's Word and his presence to keep us in the storms of life. In times when it appears we're coasting, drifting aimlessly, making one step forward and two steps backwards, it is then that we must be confident that it is not by the power of steam our equipment or even our sails. It is through the power of God.

Zechariah 4:6

⁶Then he answered and spake unto me, saying, This is the word of the LORD unto Zerubbabel, saying, Not by might, nor by power, but by my spirit, saith the LORD of hosts.

Proverbs 3:5-6

⁵Trust in the LORD with all thine heart; and lean not unto thine own understanding.⁶In all thy ways acknowledge him, and he shall direct thy paths.

It's An Absolute Must...

Time, the commodity that is given equally to all, is used differently by all and cannot be retrieved by any. It's the use of it that determines our present state, our future and our eternal destiny. The things we carve out time for in the course of our day are considered important to our well being, our progress, and our future.

So we can conclude that anything of worth will be given a block of time in our day and anything of a lesser value will be given less or no time at all. For the person who has to take dialysis treatments three times weekly, or the person who must take chemotherapy once a week, the time is not a factor, because it is a matter of life and death.

It is also a matter of life or death when an individual cannot or will not carve out one hour a week to learn the teachings, the desires and plans of God for his/her life in this world or the next. The one component required to develop a relationship or friendship is time. Time for frequent communicating, interacting and just coming to understand each other. Time must be allotted or carved out for any relationship to grow and develop into something worthwhile. Without some sacrifice, effort and value assigned to the union of your mate, family, friends, etc., the relationship status will not materialize beyond the level of an acquaintance or a casual friend. Is this how you relate to God? Is this how you relate to Jesus? Or is this how you relate to The Holy Spirit?

When the total focus is all on preparing for this materialistic world (jobs, education, homes, recreation trips, cruises cars, boats, airplanes, fashions, etc.) all these things can be wiped out in a heartbeat. When God allows us to accomplish all these earthly goals and still, one hour a week is not available to connect and advance our spiritual life, we may say with our mouth that our spiritual life is important. However, our actions are saying that it is not important, not necessary and that developing a relationship with our Heavenly Father has no benefits now or in eternity.

> ***Isaiah 55:6***
> ⁶*Seek ye the LORD while he may be found, call ye upon him while he is near.*
>
> ***Matthew 6:33***
> ³³*But seek ye first the kingdom of God, and his righteousness; and all these things shall be added unto you.*

CHAPTER TWO

Have Faith in God

Sight Unseen

The contenders for the arrival of the promised Holy Spirit probably had a very vague idea of what He would look like, resemble or how the manifestation would occur. They only had the promise that it was the Comforter, so that dispelled the fear factor which is a major concern in anything unknown. There would be nothing to expect from a loving God except a gift that would be comforting to them.

So, they waited expectantly with unwavering faith and without doubting because they trusted the One who promised. That is why they received: they believed and expected to receive; therefore they waited because He had a record, a never failing record in the past. The disciples remembered Lazarus, the Centurion's plea for the life of his son, and Peter's desperate cry for help while sinking towards a watery grave. All these recollections gave them hope that He would send the promise on time, and there was nothing to fear from the crowds downstairs trying to persuade them to leave the room, give up their weird fantasy or this unheard of hope. But they remained steadfast in their belief in the promise that Jesus would keep His Word. When Day of Pentecost was fully come, they received the promise of the Holy Ghost.

Acts 1:4-8
⁴And, being assembled together with them, commanded them that they should not depart from Jerusalem, but wait for the promise of the Father, which, saith he, ye have heard of me. ⁵For John truly baptized with water; but ye shall be baptized with the Holy Ghost not many days hence. ⁶When they therefore were come together, they asked of him, saying, Lord, wilt thou at this time restore again the kingdom to Israel? ⁷And he said unto them, It is not for you to know the times or the seasons, which the Father hath put in his own power. ⁸But ye shall receive power, after that the Holy Ghost is come upon you: and ye shall be witnesses unto me both in Jerusalem, and in all Judaea, and in Samaria, and unto the uttermost part of the earth.

Acts 2:1-4
¹And when the day of Pentecost was fully come, they were all with one accord in one place. ²And suddenly there came a sound from heaven as of a rushing mighty wind, and it filled all the house where they were sitting. ³And there appeared unto them cloven tongues like as of fire, and it sat upon each of them. ⁴And they were all filled with the Holy Ghost, and began to speak with other tongues, as the Spirit gave them utterance.

Jesus' Request: Bring Them to Me

Have you ever felt powerless? Have you ever been in a difficult situation where help does not appear to be available and there does not seem to be an end in sight? There is One who is a Savior, not only for the salvation of our souls, but Jesus Christ is our Savior in any dangerous and desperate situation we may encounter. This Savior of the universe speaks to you in your hour of need.

The father in this story had done everything humanly possible and it appeared his little son was doomed to remain demon possessed for life. As the father approached the Savior with his problem he wondered at the ineffectiveness of the disciples. Jesus issued a proclamation to him and one that is universal for every child of God. In our times of trouble, or when we experience problems, tragedies, abuses, concerns, and unsolved mysteries applicable to us today He offers the same instruction that He gave to that weary father: *Bring them to Me.*

Jesus has not changed. He still bids us to bring Me your children, your mates, your parents, your broken spirits, your failed efforts, your churches, your vice ridden communities and warring nations. Simply bring them to Him and release them.

> *Luke 9:41*
> [41]*And Jesus answering said, O faithless and perverse generation, how long shall I be with you, and suffer you? Bring thy son hither.*

Are You in the System?

Frequently, when computer operators are unable to locate information in a certain program, they remark "the information is not in the system" or "it cannot be located." Are you in the system? This does not refer to a computer system. This question asks can you be found in today's system of following traditions, customs, mores, the regular run of the mill procedures, and business as usual routines?

God through the prophet Isaiah declares that He is going to do...a new thing...something completely NEW and unheard of, something that is definitely not in the system. It is so new that there are no icons, no codes available on the present keyboards that will permit this new data entry.

The new works of God Isaiah refers to will be done by men and women of faith. Their actions will be "faith based" innovations very often misunderstood and unappreciated by family and friends. Faith based sometimes infers that policies involved in a proposal are in part based on faith in God. Funds, people, buildings, equipment, etc., are made available when a degree of faith is incorporated in a proposed document. Such people and methods can be easily located in the system. Partial faith is not God's desire.

Unlike the government, God requires one hundred percent faith in all of our actions present and future. The just shall walk by faith.

You are in the system if you are following merrily after the traditions and customs and rules of the crowd. Refusing to go along with the majority excludes one from the system or the norm. God uses methods, people and things that are not always acceptable and compatible with the norms of the day.

To know if you are in the system, you only have to ask yourself if you are so enmeshed, engrafted, and entangled in the present day customs that you fear the criticism, the quizzical expressions of those that hold today's view that, "if it feels good, do it," or the "me, myself and mine first," philosophy. If you responded positively, you are located in the system that is not entirely based on faith. Often God does not use a crowd and the crowd most often does not follow God.

Because of the way the system works, adhering to customs and traditions, God's Word becomes ineffective. Your customs and traditions will make God's Word ineffective.

Hebrews 10:38
[38]*Now the just shall live by faith: but if any man draw back, my soul shall have no pleasure in him.*

1 Corinthians 1:26-28
[26]*For ye see your calling, brethren, how that not many wise men after the flesh, not many mighty, not many noble, are called:* [27]*But God hath chosen the foolish things of the world to confound the wise; and God hath chosen the weak things of the world to confound the things which are mighty;* [28]*And base things of the world, and things which are despised, hath God chosen, yea, and things which are not, to bring to nought things that are.*

Elevate Your Thinking To A Higher Dimension

Jesus had performed the miracle of feeding the crowd of five thousand on the seashore with the lunch of a little boy. The lunch consisted of two small fish and five little loaves of bread. Following the feeding the crowd was dismissed to go home. The following day the crowd returned to the site of the miracle. Unable to locate Jesus or His disciples, they began a search. When He was found He addressed the multitude, this time addressing their motive for locating Him. He pointed out that they were not looking to receive an increase in spiritual knowledge or because they were interested in His works, but their chief concern was the hope for another miracle of multiplying food to satisfy their natural hunger.

> *John 6:26-27*
> [26]*Jesus answered them and said, Verily, verily, I say unto you, Ye seek me, not because ye saw the miracles, but because ye did eat of the loaves, and were filled.*
> [27]*Labour not for the meat which perisheth, but for that meat which endureth unto everlasting life.*

Must You Also See Before You Will Believe?

Thomas expressed his doubts to his fellow disciples, "I will not believe that He is alive unless I see and touch the wounds in His hands, feet and His side." Unaware of the omniscience of Christ, he proceeded with the discussion of the other disciples. Sometime afterwards that Sunday, Christ made His surprise visit and to Thomas' dismay, Christ sent for him and requested that he place his hands in the holes He received three days earlier.

When the will of God and the promises of God are accepted in faith, you are promised a blessing because you did not demand proof before seeing the evidence or believing God's ability to perform and deliver what He has promised. He rewards our faith in Him.

> ***John 20:25***
> ²⁵*The other disciples therefore said unto him, We have seen the LORD. But he said unto them, Except I shall see in his hands the print of the nails, and put my finger into the print of the nails, and thrust my hand into his side, I will not believe.*

Jesus Never Loses His Keys

On the third day following Christ's crucifixion, the Holy Spirit began to move in the tomb and Jesus was restored to life. He arose and began the day by folding away the clothing of his death and entombment. When this was completed He prepared to leave taking with Him the keys of death, hell and the grave. At this time He received the keys for total restoration for all things associated with death and the grave, such as sickness, incurable diseases, and hopeless accident victims, He also received keys to hell which rescues dying souls from the grips of eternal damnation.

These keys will also rescue souls in life situations that are appear to be never ending torment, hopelessness, those locked in irreconcilable relationships, insufficient finances, loss of faith and seemingly unanswered prayers.

In every situation, our focus must remain constant, never relinquishing this truth that Jesus is in complete control, and He never loses His keys; no one can steal His keys and His keys cannot be duplicated, because He has the only master set.

The Plan of God For You and Your Family

Jeremiah explains that God has plans for us as individuals and as nations. The plan does not call for anything that is harmful, dangerous or unexpected. If His people place their trust in Him, He will cause His plans to materialize in our very best interests. Jeremiah 29:11 says *"I know the plans I have for you, to do you good and not evil."*

Jesus has a plan for expectant mothers…and at no time does His plan call for you to be fearful, worried and unprotected during pregnancy nor for your future. To allow oneself to become pregnant, without the benefit of the expected child's father's involvement creates an unpredictable future for the expected baby, the future father and even the life of the expectant mother will be tremendously different from God's plan for the future of what could have been a loving family (both parents and child) and so many significant others (relatives). The absentee father can have some negative effects in the life of the child but even more unsettling is the child not knowing who or the whereabouts of the father.

When God's plan for us is not followed, the promise of receiving God's good and expected end may be interrupted or become null and void.

> *Exodus 20:14*
> *14Thou shalt not commit adultery.*
>
> *Matthew 19:4-6*
> *4And he answered and said unto them, Have ye not read, that he which made them at the beginning made them male and female, 5And said, For this cause shall a man leave father and mother, and shall cleave to his wife: and they twain shall be one flesh? 6Wherefore they are no more twain, but one flesh. What therefore God hath joined together, let not man put asunder.*
>
> *Jeremiah 29:11*
> *11For I know the thoughts that I think toward you, saith the LORD, thoughts of peace, and not of evil, to give you an expected end.*

CHAPTER THREE

Trusting God Through the Struggle

Wash Me Over Again

Without struggles, there is no progress. As surely as constant application of water washes away dirt, so constant washing (applications and instructions) in the Word washes away sin from the heart of man. The song writer petitions God to continuously wash him over again to prevent sin from creeping in again.

The constant hearing of God's Word causes our faith to increase and the constant reading of God's Word causes us to receive God's approval and become skillful in the Word.

> *Ephesians 5:26*
>
> 26*That he might sanctify and cleanse it with the washing of water by the word,*
>
> *Romans10:17*
>
> 17*So then faith cometh by hearing, and hearing by the word of God.*
>
> *2 Timothy 2:15*
>
> 15*Study to shew thyself approved unto God, a workman that needeth not to be ashamed, rightly dividing the word of truth.*

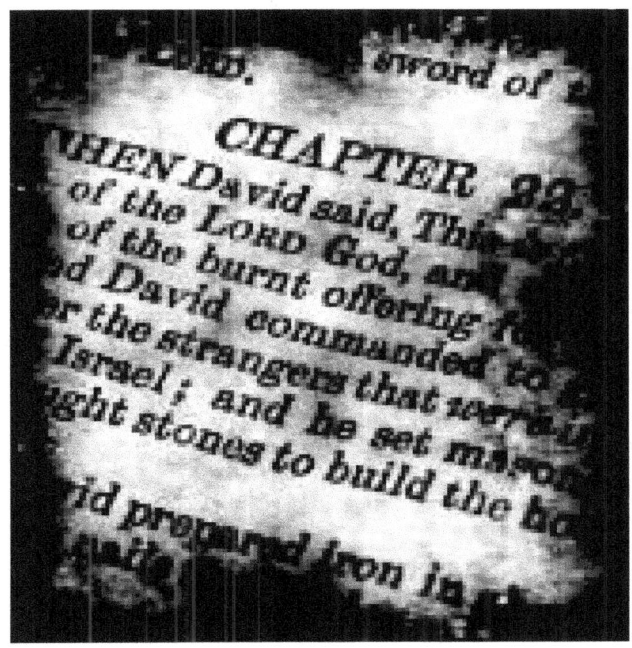

We Trusted Mom Then… But Always Trust God

Proverbs says to "Trust in the Lord with all thine heart." As a tot perhaps you fell, scratching your knee or your finger. Rushing to your mom in tears, you displayed the "severe wound" for all to see giving detailed explanation of your pain. She listened with great interest, while wiping away the little blood and soothingly cleansed, fixed it up with a kiss and she proclaimed, "It's going to be alright in a little while." Nothing further was said. *SHE* said it will be fine.

God tells us, "I am with you, I will never leave you, I will not forsake you. . .though mother and father may forsake you. . .I will not leave you until I've done what I promised. I have plans for you and no weapon formed (there's never been one that) can harm you. And this plan is still in force.

> ### Isaiah 54:17
> ¹⁷*No weapon that is formed against thee shall prosper; and every tongue that shall rise against thee in judgment thou shalt condemn. This is the heritage of the servants of the LORD, and their righteousness is of me, saith the LORD.*

Unquestionable Trust in God

A baby that wants food does not question the source of the bottle's contents. If hungry, the bottle could be given to him by a complete stranger and it will be welcomed. The baby will have no concerns about the bottle's cleanliness, temperature or correct formula amounts. The infant has no questions, nor concerns or doubts.

Without any reservations, the baby relies entirely on the caregiver to provide all of his or her needs for contentment.

This is an illustration of the trust that God wants His children to have in Him. When we make our requests known to Him, just as the baby cries out, it has trust and it has faith that "whatever is presented to me will meet my needs and it will be satisfactory."

> **Psalm 37:5**
> ⁵*Commit thy way unto the LORD; trust also in him; and he shall bring it to pass.*

There is Purpose in Our Struggle

A deceased body has to be prepared before being released for public viewing. The person may have won the award for the best physique or the Homecoming Queen. In spite of their mind boggling or sexy appeal in life, the body is not released for public viewing until certain precautions have been taken. There are some internal things (organs, etc.) that must be removed and chemical solutions must be injected into the corpse.

In the spiritual realm there are certain preparations that must be made during life in order to make the transition to see the Savior in peace. These preparations are achieved only in consistent efforts of repenting, forgiving, serving and displaying an attitude of agape love toward our fellow man and maintaining complete trust in God.

During life, there are some things that must be removed. We are told to put away everything that has the appearance of evil conduct. It is not automatic. However, the Holy Ghost will give you warnings. He will lead and guide you. We are directed to put away (stop) lying, stealing, fornicating, deceiving, etc.

In the same vein when sinful behaviors are removed they must be replaced with conduct that reflects godliness, righteousness and holiness. We must walk by faith in God's Word and not by our eyesight, hearing ability or human reasoning.

Galatians 5:13-17, 19-21, 22-26

[13]For, brethren, ye have been called unto liberty; only use not liberty for an occasion to the flesh, but by love serve one another. [14]For all the law is fulfilled in one word, even in this; Thou shalt love thy neighbour as thyself. [15]But if ye bite and devour one another, take heed that ye be not consumed one of another. [16]This I say then, Walk in the Spirit, and ye shall not fulfil the lust of the flesh. [17]For the flesh lusteth against the Spirit, and the Spirit against the flesh: and these are contrary the one to the other: so that ye cannot do the things that ye would.

[19]Now the works of the flesh are manifest, which are these; Adultery, fornication, uncleanness, lasciviousness, [20]Idolatry, witchcraft, hatred, variance, emulations, wrath, strife, seditions, heresies, [21]Envyings, murders, drunkenness, revellings, and such like: of the which I tell you before, as I have also told you in time past, that they which do such things shall not inherit the kingdom of God.

[22]But the fruit of the Spirit is love, joy, peace, longsuffering, gentleness, goodness, faith, [23]Meekness, temperance: against such there is no law. [24]And they that are Christ's have crucified the flesh with the affections and lusts. [25]If we live in the Spirit, let us also walk in the Spirit. [26]Let us not be desirous of vain glory, provoking one another, envying one another.

Your Assigned Course of Action May Be Different

Job was known as the richest man in the land of the east, but with all his riches he was unable to rid himself of the pain, misery and misfortune that that came into his life so unexpectedly. Much of his suffering came through the hands of his dearest friends and loved ones.

His closest friends came by to comfort him at a distance. Their visitation caused him great anguish and mental pain because rather than comforting, they accused him of possibly committing some great sin. Exactly what the sin or wrongdoing that he did is unclear. But it had to be something awful, because *to their thinking* God's punishment was unbelievable.

Neither these friends nor Job had knowledge of the background praise that God had given to Job and the challenge of Satan to discredit him. Therefore, they misunderstood his actions and his compliant manner because they were not aware of his unrelenting faith and trust in God. His motives and trusting relationship with God caused a temporary loss of friendship with them. Even his wife of many years offered a solution to end his suffering but because of Job's abiding faith, he refused to curse God and continued his life of seemingly unending suffering.

Job's life story ends with God's blessings of restored health and abundant wealth. It has been said that he was one patriot who received more than double for this trouble.

Job 27:6
⁶My righteousness I hold fast, and will not let it go: my heart shall not reproach me so long as I live.

Job 13:15
¹⁵Though he slay me, yet will I trust in him: but I will maintain mine own ways before him.

CHAPTER FOUR

Go and Tell the Good News!

Say What God Tells You To Proclaim

God commands the weak to say, "I am strong" and the fearful say "I am Courageous." He commanded Moses to speak to Pharaoh and say, "Let my people go." He tells Ezekiel to speak to dried, musty bones and tell them to come alive, and become active. In each of these instances, every time the man of God said the words God charged him to say, the commandment was obeyed completely in the natural down to every detail.

Pharaoh released the children of Israel and gave them riches for the journey. When Ezekiel spoke to the dry bones, they received life, breath and the activity of their limbs with great joy and praises to God.

These miracles came about by simply speaking words God commanded. We will experience the same results when we practice speaking the words God says about us in the Scriptures. God says, *"He is my father."* He says I am the righteousness of Him in Christ. (I Corinthians 1:30 Amplified) We are to believe His Word and act on it.

> *I Corinthians 1:30*
> *30But of him are ye in Christ Jesus, who of God is made unto us wisdom, and righteousness, and sanctification, and redemption:*

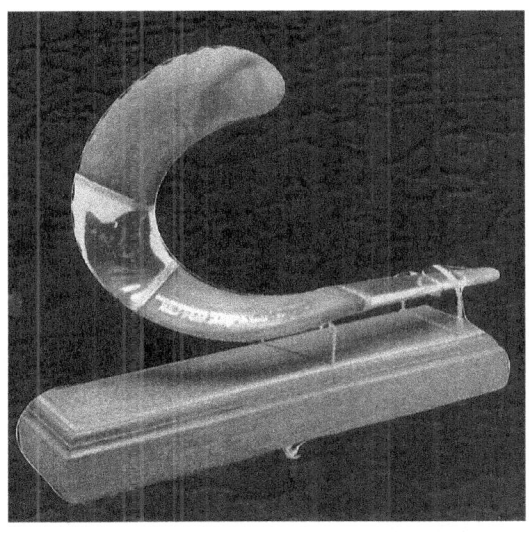

God Still Uses Teen Leaders

Focus	To begin the new year, take courage, take heart and always keep at it.
Focus Scripture	*The race is not given to the swift nor the strong, not the battle to the strong…time and chance happeneth to them all.*

Scriptural Outline		
	• The Lord is with you while you be with Him.	II Chronicles 15:2b
	• And if you seek Him	II Chronicles 7:14, Luke 11:19
	• He will be found of you;	Psalm 103:17-18
	• But if you forsake Him,	Jeremiah 9:13-16
	• He will forsake you.	Psalm 89:11-14
	• So be strong	II Chronicles 15:7

- Let not your hands be weak   Isaiah 35:4

This young man's' rule was forty years and in the Bible he was spoken of as doing that, "which was good and right in the eyes of the Lord, his God." I Kings 15:11-14. He was also remembered as, "the king with the perfect heart all his days." He died with a disease of the feet and II Chronicles 16, at the end of the chapter it is stated that he sought not help from God but from the physicians. We can conclude that God was with him, prospered him and made him victorious all the while he was with God.

In conclusion, the beginning of the race may be outstanding, but the scores are not tallied until the race ends. At any minute the speed may pick up, the distance increase, and the tension intensifies but don't relax your grip, stay focused, stay in the race until you reach the goal because God will be with you as long as you're with him.

KEYS TO SUCCESS WITH GOD'S APPROVAL

Give and it shall be given back to you (multiplied many times over)

Do things for others that you would want them to do for you.

You shall reap the same things in your life that you're sowing into the lives of others.

Treat your friends as they're family members and treat your family like they're friends.

CHAPTER FIVE

Accept What He Has to Offer

The Wise Gladly Accept Wisdom

Speed traps are secluded spots along busy thoroughfares and highways where traffic patrolmen frequently park in effort to catch traffic violators. Frequent travelers along those routes are usually happy to caution drivers of these hideouts along certain familiar roads. Youngsters or strangers unfamiliar with the area can avoid the sudden pullovers and the expensive traffic tickets by giving heed to the older traveler's advice which was gained through their experience.

Rehoboam was a young man who became king in Israel. It was an honorable gesture for him to seek wisdom from advisors for ruling the great kingdom. He received advice from the wise men who had served his father. He then he asked the advice of his peers.

After hearing both groups, he decided to discount the advice of his elders and follow the harsh suggestions of his peers who were unfamiliar with the hidden pitfalls that would be the result of a ruler's rash decisions such as they proposed. By rejecting the wisdom of aged and experienced leaders, his reign was not a time of peace and it was also short lived.

1 Kings 12:6-11
6And king Rehoboam consulted with the old men, that stood before Solomon his father while he yet lived, and said, How do ye advise that I may answer this people? 7And they spake unto him, saying, If thou wilt be a servant unto this people this day, and wilt serve them, and answer them, and speak good words to them, then they will be thy servants for ever. 8But he forsook the counsel of the old men, which they had given him, and consulted with the young men that were grown up with him, and which stood before him: 9And he said unto them, What counsel give ye that we may answer this people, who have spoken to me, saying, Make the yoke which thy father did put upon us lighter? 10And the young men that were grown up with him spake unto him, saying, Thus shalt thou speak unto this people that spake unto thee, saying, Thy father made our yoke heavy, but make thou it lighter unto us; thus shalt thou say unto them, My little finger shall be thicker than my father's loins. 11And now whereas my father did lade you with a heavy yoke, I will add to your yoke: my father hath chastised you with whips, but I will chastise you with scorpions.
Proverbs 13:10
10Only by pride cometh contention: but with the well advised is wisdom.
Proverbs 19:20
20Hear counsel, and receive instruction, that thou mayest be wise in thy latter end.

Jesus Accepts Your Works Following Your Relationship

Most of us have seen an old familiar face standing before us with a big smile calling out our name with great excitement. We recalled the face with equal delight but the embarrassment could not be hidden. While giving a brisk handshake asking, "When did we see each other last?" trying to make a relational connection. After the old friend reminds you of the great times you have had together, you are still pitifully blank. When the time comes that you have an encounter with Jesus, will you have to recount events and occasions to jog His memory so as to recall that last time so long ago that you spent with him, just the two of you or will He say, "I don't know you."

The world cannot understand most of the spiritual truths as they are not received on the same frequency waves. God's Word is not discerned by ears that that are not listening or receptive in certain environments. The messages are not received in dead zones.

An individual can be in the same room or yard with a puppy and the pet will become alert because it hears in a distance a siren that is inaudible to human ears. The closer the siren approaches the more the pet will be disturbed because the high pitched sounds causes discomfort to the ears of dogs and other animals such as bats, birds etc. Because they are physically unable to hear such high pitched sounds humans are not affected.

Many things God speaks to one individual cannot be understood or even heard by another standing beside them. Therefore, your directions from God may be indelibly imprinted in your mind, but totally unthinkable to another to the extent that they would discourage you from carrying out a task God has destined only for you. (The prophet was told to return home by a different route. He was persuaded by what seemed to be a well meaning friend who gave him bad advice. His life was lost by disobedience. Although his mission was completed, it was disastrous because he did not obey God's instructions completely. He was persuaded to divert from the original instructions given by God.)

> **1 Kings 13:7**
> ⁷And the king said unto the man of God, Come home with me, and refresh thyself, and I will give thee a reward.

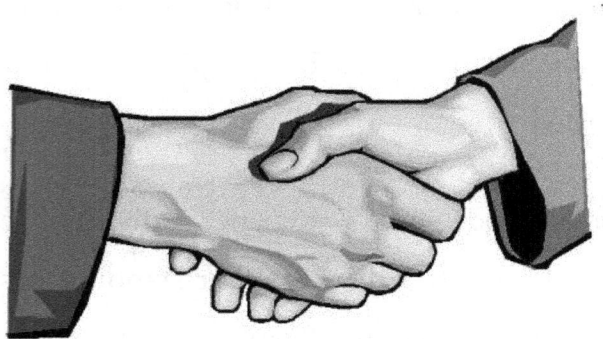

CHAPTER SIX

He Offers World Wide Coverage

The Sufficiency of God

This morning you did not think it necessary to ask God for fresh air to breathe; as Americans we did not have to ask for clean water. As you moved about in your home, it did not occur to you to ask for heat and light from the sun to warm your body, to nourish the earth, the animals and plants of the earth.

Perhaps, you have not felt the need to petition God for these absolute necessities because they've always been there for us. He has always supplied those necessities for us, and true to His promise every need that you and I have, He promises to supply. Because of this we need to show our gratitude as we have been taught to say "Thank You" when anything is given to us.

> **Philippians 4:19**
> ¹⁹But my God shall supply all your need according to his riches in glory by Christ Jesus.

No Questions, Just Do It!

The main character in this Scripture passage is Naaman a powerful leader in Syria, who was also a leper. He felt uncomfortable following the instructions of a little hired servant girl. The little servant girl had knowledge the leper had not been privy to. She had firsthand experience from her hometown of a man who was anointed from God to pray for healing and shared it with Naaman.

Naaman was reluctant to receive the suggestion, partly because of his ego. Those standing by saw at the little girl was about to be dismissed and they joined her by telling the leper, "there's nothing to lose if you try but, if you don't try, you could lose everything to this disease." After much persuasion he arrived at the prophet's gate but his attitude was unchanged. Again he rejected the words of deliverance. Naaman was dissatisfied because

- *Elisha did not come out to greet him*
- *The river Jordan was muddy*
- *Elisha failed to pray over him*
- *Overall was critical of his prophetic abilities until he was convinced by his servants to follow Elisha's instructions*

Many times, as God's servants, we find ourselves in places where we are both misunderstood and in the minority. We hold the key to deliverance for God's children who are without the knowledge of His Word and promises are available just for the asking.

With much conflict, the great leader realized his healing would not have occurred without the courageous persuasions of the humble servant who shared her knowledge of *her God*. When he changed his attitude and obeyed the prophet's instructions, his flesh became as clean as a baby.

II Kings 5:1-14

¹Now Naaman, captain of the host of the king of Syria, was a great man with his master, and honourable, because by him the LORD had given deliverance unto Syria: he was also a mighty man in valour, but he was a leper. ²And the Syrians had gone out by companies, and had brought away captive out of the land of Israel a little maid; and she waited on Naaman's wife. ³And she said unto her mistress, Would God my lord were with the prophet that is in Samaria! for he would recover him of his leprosy. ⁴And one went in, and told his lord, saying, Thus and thus said the maid that is of the land of Israel. ¹¹But Naaman was wroth... So he turned and went away in a rage. ¹³And his servants came near, and spake unto him, and said, My father, if the prophet had bid thee do some great thing, wouldest thou not have done it? how much rather then, when he saith to thee, Wash, and be clean? ¹⁴Then went he down, and dipped himself seven times in Jordan, according to the saying of the man of God: and his flesh came again like unto the flesh of a little child, and he was clean.

CHAPTER SEVEN

It's Your Choice

Thoughts are Seeds for Action

The battle worn soldier tried desperately to calm the wounded comrade who moaned in pain. He had sustained numerous injuries, and was slowly losing blood and vital fluids. In between the moans he continued begging his buddies to remove his boots.

Fearful he would be heard by nearby enemies, they did everything in their power to keep him quiet, but nothing stopped his tearful pleading to take off his boots and to relieve his misery. His fellow soldiers realized he was losing consciousness and was "talking out of his head." They tried soothing him with comforting words, but he refused to be quieted and continued his mournful sounds. Fearing for their lives in enemy territory one soldier suggested to a buddy, that he "do it." The other buddy said, "I can't do it, you do it." No one wanted to do it.

What was so difficult about removing a wounded friend's boots? Taking off the boots of a dying friend would have been easy except there were no boots. His legs were severed from the knees down and his feet had been lost in action. They were so ashamed. Ashamed of their thoughts, not of what they did or did not do. They were ashamed and they suffered for the thoughts they had of "putting him out of his misery." Their thinking violated the seventh commandment, *Thou shall not kill.* Euthanasia, sometimes called mercy killing, is not a biblical option. Such thinking should not be entertained, because God is mankind's only Source for life and death.

> ***Deuteronomy 5:17***
> *Thou shalt not kill.*

Lost Opportunity

Should your church or a district in your reformation encounter problems and the membership begins to dwindle, how do you respond in your heart? Although you may not be directly involved, do you feel that you share some of the blame? Do you ask yourself any of the following questions –

- Did I take every opportunity to avert this pain in the body of Christ?
- As a church official or leader in any capacity did I demonstrate passion in fulfilling my ministry assignment or was I "just doing my job?"
- Could I have thrown out the life line and helped to resolve the problem?

It only takes one individual at the helm of the largest ship to change its course and you are one individual. Let us consider a family that is the topic of everyone's discussion list.

- The family breaks up
- Or a son or daughter is killed

Do we as church leaders dismiss the family pain with a shrug of the shoulder and think, "how sad?" Is there something that probes our heart as we recall the last time we spent with them, asking ourselves if just maybe we hadn't been so rushed, we could have heard the anguish, saw the sadness, prayed with them, and availed ourselves in some way that would have prevented this outcome?

Perhaps, that last lesson we studied in YWCC (or young women's) class would have encouraged her to think beyond the present and hold fast to life in Christ. You may think, "if only I had tried harder to get the Purity Class (or teen class) off the ground…they are so anxious to be involved. The only request is that we meet monthly or bi-monthly and I have been given the lesson for the entire year. It could be the husband would have come back to the Marriage Enrichment session if we'd pressed in to be consistent with our meeting schedules." You may think, "Lord, I'd give anything to turn the clock back just a few weeks, for another opportunity but I don't have that power. It is now another lost opportunity.

It is my prayer, "that You will forgive me and help me to remember that a position and holding an office in the organization or the church is more than having a title, raising funds or having space on the program. It is a task to be executed among Your children. They have eternal souls that need the fellowship and encouragement from the Word, regularly.

Those men in the twenty-fifth chapter of St. Matthew were given bags (talents) of gold by their master. One was issued five bags, another three bags and the last man received one bag of gold. At the master's request to return the gold he found that the first two men doubled the gold. Therefore, the master was happy with their productivity and increased them. The third man hid his gold, did not invest it, so there was no increase. The one bag of gold was taken from him and he was described by his master as lazy, wicked and a worthless servant. The master further commanded that he would be thrown into outer darkness, where there would be *weeping and gnashing of teeth.*

We see in this passage of Scripture that the Lord requires productivity, effectiveness and faith accompanied with your work (action). It is not the size of the talent (the bag of gold), it is the use of the opportunity and the faithfulness to the master's call of service. Are your works overshadowed with lame excuses and complaints beginning with, "they won't, I tried, but they don't...?" You can change your mindset with God to overshadow your excuses with faith actions and a diligent determination to succeed.

Mary the mother of Jesus said to the servers, *"whatsoever he saith unto you, do it..."*

> ### Mark 16:15
> *And he said unto them. Go ye into all the world , and preach the gospel to every creature.*
>
> ### James 1:22
> *But be ye doers of the word, and not hearers only, deceiving your own selves.*
>
> ### James 4:17
> *Therefore to him that knoweth to do good, and doeth it not, to him it is a sin.*

CHAPTER EIGHT

The Unlimited Power of God

Run Boy Run
(Lil Sis)

Wilma Rudolph, born prematurely, couldn't walk which necessitated that she wear braces. Her physical challenges were blamed on her premature birth but with great determination, she overcame her disabilities and at age 16 became the youngest member of the U.S. Olympics Team. She was later inducted in the U.S. Olympics Hall of Fame because at an early age she refused to accept handicaps, hold backs, and pitiful names. Instead she said "give me the baton," and I will run.

Much like the relay races Rudolph championed, we are all in a relay race, where one runs a distance and when you complete the distance you must pass the baton to the next person who is waiting in the line to continue the race toward victory. As long as the baton (the task, the job, the assignment, the position held, the appointment, etc.) is in your possession you must run with it. As Paul challenged, run the race with patience and don't look back at prematurity, underdeveloped muscles, limbs and not even the lack of the skills can be used as excuses. An old adage, for encouragement and persistence, states "he who makes excuses seldom makes anything else."

The runner must not slack the pace, nor look left or right but run the race that is set, laid out and marked for him/her. Run Little Sister, Run Big Sister or Run Baby Sister has nothing to do with size, age, looks, education, race or religion. Everyone has a race set before them according to their God given innate abilities and talents. You must carry the baton as the runner with nothing else in your hands except the baton. Your hands as well as your mind must be free, without unnecessary weights, extra agendas or attachments to the world. When you commit to run this race, Christ fires the gun, and all of your burdens are with Him, because He contracts to meet all your needs.

As the track runner, every muscle in your body is propelling you forward. Your jaws are filled with wind which the lungs require and the veins in your neck and temples are bulging, sweat flows freely from your brow to your feet. Tiredness is overruled, body pain is outweighed. The runner has only one thought...win the race, the winner's crown.

The race against the enemy of your soul must be run with such a level of commitment realizing you're not in the race alone but the Spirit of God is empowering you to win!

2 Samuel 23:10
10He arose, and smote the Philistines until his hand was weary, and his hand clave unto the sword: and the LORD wrought a great victory that day; and the people returned after him only to spoil.

When God Clears the Way

Everyone has had experiences where you realize that you're having a *God intervention*. You can recall the time you were determined to be on time for an event, but a couple interruptions in your schedule, and suddenly you see driving time will not allow you to arrive at your destination on time. You are acutely aware of all the tension and depressing feelings that accompany being late and the sick feelings because you're late again. As you pull out the drive you know you'll never make it. As you enter onto the main thoroughfare, you prepare to break for the traffic light and then the lights are green and every lane is free. You silently offer thanks. Several blocks away you can see the light is green but you can't figure out how long it's been on green so you slow your speed expecting a caution signal. It remains green and you move on through. There's still a two or three miles and heavy traffic areas ahead, and you can't believe your eyes, but all the lights are saying go!

Driving onto the freeway ramp it looks like you will not be just too late, time flies, and it's time to exit off. You say to yourself hallelujah that light was green! You glance at the clock and there's going to be enough time to park, but the lot seems full, and the uneasy feelings begin. You see a car backing out! You wait, park, rush in the building bursting with grateful praise because God did it. He cleared the way. All things worked for your good! In everyday life, we'll never know the times God sent his angels to intervene on our behalf. Sometimes circumstances are prearranged so that all obstacles are removed and all of our paths are cleared. At other times we are left in situations that are humanly impossible to maneuver, without His help, but He always clears the way.... and lo, I am with you always.

> *Hebrews 13:5*
> 5*Let your conversation be without covetousness; and be content with such things as ye have: for he hath said, I will never leave thee, nor forsake thee.*

Today is the Day...

Time is short, always advancing, and never standing still. You are one day closer to the end of your life than you were on yesterday. Jesus lived with this thought, realizing the time to complete His earthly tasks was limited. Therefore, when the disciples asked Him about the man who was born blind, if the parents of the man had committed sin, Jesus responded, *we must work the works of Him that sent Me as long as it is day, night is coming and no man can work.* For those of us in the 21st century, the works that He was given have now become our works.

The pronoun "we" implies a team effort. Each of us as team members have been given a very narrow window of time to complete the work He has assigned to us. We then are workers together with Him. "I beseech you also that ye received not the grace of God in vain...Behold now is the accepted time, behold, now is the day of salvation." 2 Corinthians 6:1-2b

> *John 9:4 NASV*
> *We must work the works of Him who sent Me as long as it is day; night is coming when no one can work.*

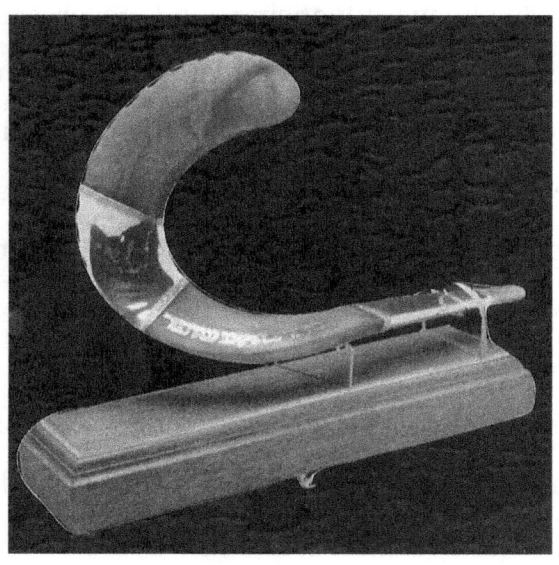

CHAPTER NINE

Service Agreements

The Way to Go

When a person is physically lost, they are unsure and definitely do not know their whereabouts, so they will seek someone to show them how to find the way to their desired location.

An individual that recognizes he is spiritually lost also needs someone to show him how to find the way to Jesus who is *the* way. There are no other directions available. There is only one way to avoid being lost and ending up in hell and Jesus is that way.

Many homes have gated entrances, some may be fenced in and some feature impressive doorways. In order to see God in eternal peace there is no architectural structure for an entranceway on the building plan. You cannot enter as one passes a sensor and the door opens automatically. Jesus stands as the only door (or entranceway) to the Father. He is now inviting you to come to Him. *Jesus saith unto him, I am the way, the truth, and the life: no man cometh unto the Father, but by me. John 14:6*

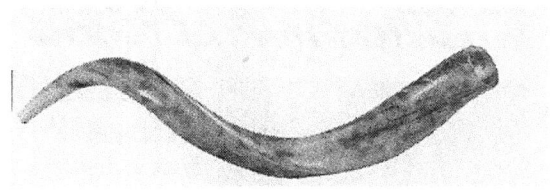

John 14:6

6Jesus saith unto him, I am the way, the truth, and the life: no man cometh unto the Father, but by me.

Matthew 1:21

And she shall bring forth a son, and they shall call his name Jesus: for he shall save his people from their sins.

The Wages For Sin
vs.
The Gift of God

Wages are the pay check received for work done for another. The wages for sin, unrighteous living, an ungodly lifestyle and unjust and immoral behaviors in biblical times required the death (a blood sacrifice) of an animal meeting certain specified qualifications. That blood sacrifice was the only avenue (payment) to receiving forgiveness for sin.

Today, payment of an animal blood sacrifice is unacceptable because God's Son was born into the world as the only sacrifice acceptable to Him. Jesus Christ was crucified, shedding His blood on the cross of Calvary for salvation, the forgiveness of sin worldwide and healing for the body, mind and soul. Unlimited coverage for every sin committed is available for all people.

God does not require any payment or purchase from you. When you accept what Jesus has done on the cross, you are then ready to receive *the gift of God, that is, eternal life (all sin paid in full).*

Hebrews 10:1, 4-5, 14-18

[1] For the law having a shadow of good things to come, and not the very image of the things, can never with those sacrifices which they offered year by year continually make the comers thereunto perfect.

[4] For it is not possible that the blood of bulls and of goats should take away sins. [5] Wherefore when he cometh into the world, he saith, Sacrifice and offering thou wouldest not, but a body hast thou prepared me.

[14] For by one offering he hath perfected for ever them that are sanctified. [15] Whereof the Holy Ghost also is a witness to us: for after that he had said before, [16] This is the covenant that I will make with them after those days, saith the Lord, I will put my laws into their hearts, and in their minds will I write them; [17] And their sins and iniquities will I remember no more. [18] Now where remission of these is, there is no more offering for sin.

Romans 6:23

[23] For the wages of sin is death; but the gift of God is eternal life through Jesus Christ our Lord.

2 Peter 2:15, 17-19

[15] Which have forsaken the right way, and are gone astray... [17] These are wells without water, clouds that are carried with a tempest; to whom the mist of darkness is reserved for ever. [18] For when they speak great swelling words of vanity, they allure through the lusts of the flesh, through much wantonness, those that were clean escaped from them who live in error. [19] While they promise them liberty, they themselves are the servants of corruption: for of whom a man is overcome, of the same is he brought in bondage.

God's Amen

Have you been reading a book and it was so enjoyable that as you approached the ending, you regretted the end was near? When you recognized there was only one page left, you delayed turning to that last page. In our lives there are some things we dread and we are reluctant to go to the next stage.

Most funerals we attend, God has said amen to the life of the deceased, but to the family and friends that remain He has graciously said, "to be continued." That represents an extension of time to complete an assignment or even one task, before He proclaims "amen" for those He allowed to remain.

It may be something as simple as a visit or a few visits, a phone call, a text message, a bridge in a relationship that needs mending and you are the only source of material God wants to use. There may very well be a song in you, only you, a painting, a vision that has not been proclaimed or perhaps a little broken child that is waiting for your caring touch.

Whatever the task or assignment it must be remembered that sufficient time will be allotted. When it is exhausted, your book of life will end and God's Amen will close it. *It is appointed unto man once to die....and after this, the judgment.* No one will plead your case. God will be before you as the Judge. As you read these words, the Spirit of God is pleading with you to set your house in order, get your affairs together, do the work that He has placed within your heart to accomplish. It may not appear to be successful to you. You are not instructed to be successful, but you're instructed to put your heart into your work and He promises to be with you and bless your work.

> ***John 9:4***
> *4I must work the works of him that sent me, while it is day: the night cometh, when no man can work.*

The Night is Coming

No one has ever been able to harness time. Man cannot stop the advancement of time nor can he turn it backwards. It cannot be sped up nor can it be slowed down. This is one of the forces in life over which man has no control. There have been times you had a good dream and you wished you could extend time so the dream could continue. The other extreme would be the experiencing of a bad dream where the dream seems too long, resulting in a night of unrest. When the morning alarm sounds, either way the extension of time is an absolute impossibility.

In the daylight hours, no matter how wonderful it has been, the night is advancing and cannot be stopped for any reason. Not even death can stop it from advancing. Night is not always considered the second half of the p.m. on the face of the clock. Night can be those times in life when you would give anything if you could ask someone to, "hold back the night," everything seems hopeless, bleak, and bland. Although it is high noon and the light of day is at its brightest, there is no joy. Laughter is a special event for one experiencing a night season. Your voice expresses lack of enthusiasm, it has no pep and your face would never be in the happy face contest.

This is a picture of a person whose night is coming and they have surrendered to its clutches. They are not surrendered to trust in God, not realizing that He is the only one that has stopped time and even made time stand still. He is in full control of the approaching night in all our lives. The announcement of an incurable disease, the sentence of death for a loved one, the statement, " I want a divorce, my child was sent home with a letter from the nurse, stating she is pregnant, he or she was dead on arrival. These are examples of announcements that one may receive in the morning or even at lunch, when the sun is shining at its brightest, but suddenly it is as though it is midnight and the lights are off.

You are in a state of utter confusion, pandemonium, and you can only feel your way, sometime, stumbling and even falling.

Jesus Christ, God's Son, can make life in the night season a relative joy, because He is the light of your night season. Total surrender to Him will cause the darkness and all its descriptions to be as the brightness of noonday and everything is perfect because in Him, with Him and through Him, there is no (existence of) darkness.

> ### Psalm 139:12
> 12 Yea, the darkness hideth not from thee; but the night shineth as the day: the darkness and the light are both alike to thee.
>
> ### Isaiah 5:20
> 20 Woe unto them that call evil good, and good evil; that put darkness for light, and light for darkness; that put bitter for sweet, and sweet for bitter!
>
> ### I John 1:5-7
> 5 This then is the message which we have heard of him, and declare unto you, that God is light, and in him is no darkness at all. 6 If we say that we have fellowship with him, and walk in darkness, we lie ,and do not the truth: 7 But if we walk in the light,, as he is in the light, we have fellowship one with another, and the blood of Jesus Christ his Son cleanseth as us from all sin.

CHAPTER TEN

Your Faithfulness Commends You to God

The Only Choice is the Right Choice

If Christ has control of the mind, your mindset is not to react negatively to another's unacceptable behavior, because you cannot accept responsibility for their actions. When an offender commits an offense toward you, you must decide how you will respond. You are only accountable for your responses to them. There are many choices that will come to mind, but there is only one right choice....Forgive the offender and...*Do It Now*.

> **Ephesians 4:32**
> ³²*And be ye kind one to another, tenderhearted, forgiving one another, even as God for Christ's sake hath forgiven you.*
>
> **Colossians 3:13**
> ¹³*Forbearing one another, and forgiving one another, if any man have a quarrel against any: even as Christ forgave you, so also do ye.*

God is Omnipresent

When we call for or invite Jesus into our presence we desire an answer to our prayer request or to visibly see evidence of change. So we resort to calling Him or inviting Him to come where we are located.

We must realize that He is omnipresent, we do not need to call Him to come because He is already there in our midst, wherever we are. If you're in the depths of hell, on the highest mountain, at the ocean bottom or the farthest corner of the earth…He is there. He is omnipresent. He is everywhere.

Psalm 139:7-12

⁷Whither shall I go from thy spirit? or whither shall I flee from thy presence? ⁸If I ascend up into heaven, thou art there: if I make my bed in hell, behold, thou art there. ⁹If I take the wings of the morning, and dwell in the uttermost parts of the sea; ¹⁰Even there shall thy hand lead me, and thy right hand shall hold me. ¹¹If I say, Surely the darkness shall cover me; even the night shall be light about me. ¹²Yea, the darkness hideth not from thee; but the night shineth as the day: the darkness and the light are both alike to thee.

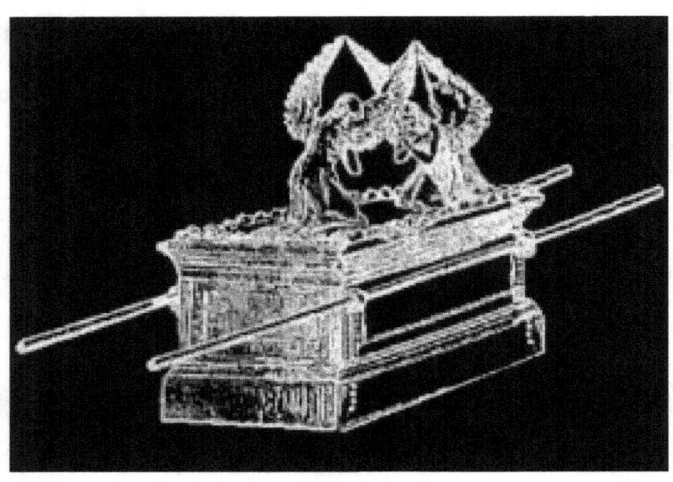

The Supernatural Power of Christ

The supernatural powers of Christ were affirmed by many citizens in the villages and towns of His day. His abilities to heal sicknesses and even deliver from death caused them to understand that He was more than a prophet.

In describing Himself, He said "I am the resurrection and the life. He that believeth on me though He were dead, yet shall he live." The gentleman whose daughter was at home several furlongs away suggested that Jesus should not come to his home; the power of His Word was such that He could speak to her body from the distance and she would be healed. Jesus did speak to her illness and she was healed at that instant.

Martha, the sister of Mary (who anointed Jesus' body for the crucifixion), expressed her faith in the limitless power of Christ by saying to Him, *"Lord I know if thou had been here, my brother would not have died. And even now, whatsoever you ask of God, He will give it thee."* And if you believe, He will respond today the same way for you.

> *Matthew 8:8*
> ⁸*The centurion answered and said, Lord, I am not worthy that thou shouldest come under my roof: but speak the word only, and my servant shall be healed.*
> *Matthew 8:13*
> ¹³*And Jesus said unto the centurion, Go thy way; and as thou hast believed, so be it done unto thee. And his servant was healed in the selfsame hour.*

Healing Is A Process

A scab on a wound is the sign that the break in the skin is gone and underneath healing is almost complete. You should not attempt to move the scab, when it has nothing further to protect underneath, it will drop off. You may not be aware that it is gone, but one day you will look at the area and realize that the healing process is finished.

In life, broken promises sometimes seem unforgettable. Additionally, expected apologies are not given and broken hearts seem so shattered they can feel like a beautiful puzzle nearly complete, but just two or three pieces are missing. In such situations the only hope for one in such a state of mind is to trust God and pray for His unfailing divine strength to forgive the offender.

Like the scab on the broken skin, continued prayer and expectant faith will cause the emotional healing process to advance until it is totally complete. Unobserved by you, the pain and hurt that was so intense some months or years ago is now gone. With faith and consistent prayer, the disappointment, the betrayal, the lies of denial and rejection no longer seem important. Their significance like the scab just fell away, without any further pain. There was nothing more to cover and protect, the healing process was completed by God.

> *Colossians 3:13*
> *Forbearing one another, and forgiving one another, if any man have a quarrel against any; even as Christ forgave you, so also do ye.*
>
> *Matthew 6:14-15*
> *14 For if ye forgive men their trespass, your heavenly Father will also forgive you: 15 But if ye forgive not men their trespasses, neither will your Father forgive your trespasses.*

Life and Death Are in Our Words

One of the greatest enemies to a person striving to live a godly life is the mouth. It expresses the issues of the heart and is so powerful that it can be the beginning or the first step toward ending great wars among nations, gangs within cities and irreconcilable family feuds.

Once words are uttered they cannot be recalled, however, they can be repented of and forgiven. When one asks forgiveness or offers an apology, few acts are more like the humility of Christ. And it is at this point that the deceptive enemy would suggest resistance because Satan would have the offender believe, it is not that "big a thing" or that he/she would become smaller or less important in the eyes of others. The fact is the offender who spoke out of term would appear quite the opposite to onlookers. This graceful act would be a Christlike example of spiritual maturity. If a person hates to apologize for whatever reasons, but desires to live a righteous life, they must constantly guard their words and not be ruled by their mouth. Failure to consistently guard (keep the gates of the mouth closed) will result in the need for much Christlike repentance and humbling apologies.

To neglect this essential character building lesson opens the door for the enemy to gain access to hinder your living a victorious life. Your living, teaching, preaching, and soul winning efforts will be overshadowed by that one time you walked away trying to feel big, important and in charge. Such lessons overlooked will not allow you to testify, teach or lead discussions on the grace of God. When one do not recognize the lessons you may also fail to act with humility even when in the right as Christ's example at the cross of Calvary or to acknowledge and apologize when undecidedly another has been wounded by your impatient, unkind and hurtful words.

In order for God to receive the glory, for us to live an overcoming and victorious life, we must determine daily that we will not be ruled by our mouths.

Proverbs 16:24
Pleasant words are as an honeycomb, sweet to the soul, and health to the bones.

Ecclesiastes 9:17
The words of wise men are heard in quiet more than the cry of him that ruleth among fools.

Psalm 39:1
I said, I will take heed to my ways, that I sin not with my tongue: I will keep my mouth with a bridle, while the wicked is before me.

Psalm 34:1
1I will bless the LORD at all times: his praise shall continually be in my mouth.

1 Timothy 6:3-5
3If any man teach otherwise, and consent not to wholesome words, even the words of our Lord Jesus Christ, and to the doctrine which is according to godliness; 4He is proud, knowing nothing, but doting about questions and strifes of words, whereof cometh envy, strife, railings, evil surmisings, 5Perverse disputings of men of corrupt minds, and destitute of the truth, supposing that gain is godliness: from such withdraw thyself.

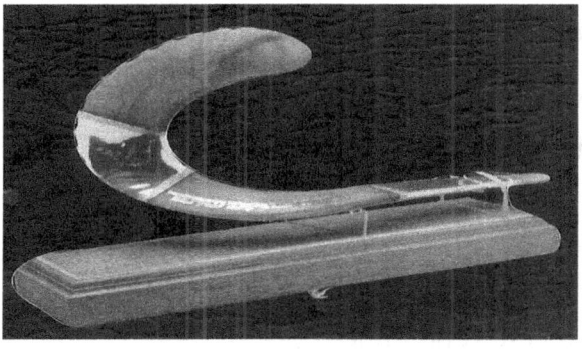

Satan: The Accuser of the Brethren

Okay, so you committed a sin at eight thirty this morning. Immediately the Spirit of God prompts you to repent, but suddenly you have this thought that you've already blown the day so there is no need to repent at this juncture. That was the voice of the enemy discouraging your repentance. He does this so that he may continue accusing you with thoughts that you have already, "done that" or perhaps, "too bad you've already said that." His push is to steer us away from God.

Jesus wants us to remember there is no sin that He will not forgive with sincere repentance.

Isaiah 55:6-7

⁶ Seek ye the Lord while he may be found. Call ye upon him while he is near: ⁷ Let the wicked forsake his way, and the unrighteous man his thoughts: and let him return unto the LORD, and he will have mercy; and to our God, for he will abundantly pardon.

2 Corinthians 6:2

For he saith, I have heard thee in a time accepted, and in the day of salvation have I succoured thee: behold, now is the accepted time, behold, now is the day of salvation.

2 Peter 3:9-12

⁹The Lord is not slack concerning his promise, as some men count slackness; but is longsuffering to us-ward, not willing that any should perish, but that all should come to repentance.

¹⁰But the day of the Lord will come as a thief in the night; in the which the heavens shall pass away with a great noise, and the elements shall melt with fervent heat, the earth also and the works that are therein shall be burned up.

¹¹Seeing then that all these things shall be dissolved, what manner of persons ought ye to be in all holy conversation and godliness, ¹²Looking for and hasting unto the coming of the day of God, wherein the heavens being on fire shall be dissolved, and the elements shall melt with fervent heat?

CHAPTER ELEVEN

Rid Yourself of the Negative and Accept God's Love

Sabotage

Sabotage – A Device of the enemy of the Soul to bring one to spiritual destruction. *(Walking in the flesh)*

Righteousness – Works of unfeigned love in much patience and faith in God for glorious victory. *(Walking in the Spirit)*

These all endured sabotage at the evil hands of the enemy:
- *Joseph (Suffered at the hands of "the brotherhood", his eleven brothers)*
- *Nehemiah (Suffered at the hands Sanballat)*
- *David (Suffered at the hands of the leader Saul and <u>his</u> own son, Absalom)*
- *Adam/Eve (Suffered at the hands of Satan)*

The greatest sabotage attempt was on Jesus by the High Priest and the courts but He refused to turn around. He continued on through the crowd up the hill, to obtain the victory on Calvary.

> *Isaiah 30:15*
>
> ¹⁵*For thus saith the Lord GOD, the Holy One of Israel; In returning and rest shall ye be saved; in quietness and in confidence shall be your strength: and ye would not.*

God's Extraordinary Love

When the sacrificial payment for errors of sin added up to more than the sinner's finances would allow, God placed a plan in operation that eliminated the entire process of animal sacrifices. God's plan was as easy as a mental willingness to accept the one sacrifice He provided in the Lamb of God, His Son Jesus. He also placed into operation a miraculous plan that provided that those in the Christian walk would never be alone anymore. Though unseen they are always accompanied by the unseen presence of the Holy Spirit.

With the work of Christ on the cross, and the operation of the

Holy Spirit, God's great love included yet another phase. In the event sin tried to regain a foothold, Christ our Advocate provides us with a petition or prayer for forgiveness. He is always with us.

> **John 14:17-18**
> *17Even the Spirit of truth; whom the world cannot receive, because it seeth him not, neither knoweth him: but ye know him; for he dwelleth with you, and shall be in you. 18I will not leave you comfortless: I will come to you.*
>
> *Psalm 103:2-3*
>
> *Bless the Lord, O my soul, and forget not all his benefits: Who forgiveth all thine iniquities; who healeth all thy diseases.*

You Can't Beat God "Giving"

Jesus took the bread and fish that were collected and said a prayer of thanks. He multiplied one little lunch to feed five thousand people plus the women and children. Everything you give to Christ, no matter how small, will be blessed, multiplied and returned back to the giver.

Unless a grain of wheat falls to the ground and dies, the only wheat you'll ever have will remain in the seed bag or seed container. But if the seed is removed from the owner's container and is sown or shared with another, it is then in the spiritual position to bring forth more fruit which will be multiplied back to the giver.

> **Luke 6:38**
> ³⁸*Give, and it shall be given unto you; good measure, pressed down, and shaken together, and running over, shall men give into your bosom. For with the same measure that ye mete withal it shall be measured to you again.*

Vessels With Special Design and Time

Some of the most common mix-ups in life today can found in the postal system, packages delivered to incorrect addresses, grade mistakes in schools and colleges, and infrequently in hospital operation rooms. Our faith in God is error free. He never needs the strike over key, the delete button or the eraser, because He is God. And He never makes mistakes.

Our dates of birth and death are settled and his plans and designs for our individual lives are also established. The expected outcome and all that occurs "in between" according to

His design is not a surprise to Him but a definite part of His design and anticipated results for each of us.

> *Jeremiah 29:11-13*
>
> ¹¹For I know the thoughts that I think toward you, saith the LORD, thoughts of peace, and not of evil, to give you an expected end. ¹²Then shall ye call upon me, and ye shall go and pray unto me, and I will hearken unto you. ¹³And ye shall seek me, and find me, when ye shall search for me with all your heart.

"Can You Do Me A Favor?"

I need some help, "can you do me a favor?" This is a very common expression used when the speaker is requesting that you would meet an urgent need for him/her. If one responds in the positive, no matter how great the need is or the time the favor is to be delivered, the favor is expected.

When God gives favor, it is not a onetime gift. To have His favor circumstances, conditions and even situations are always favorably aligned for success. Favor from God is not expected, not requested, but it is just another blessing from the Lord, expressing His love. The favor of God will make you look good. With God's favor you are "marked to make it."

God's favor has the tendency to show special kindness, approval or unexpected preference. Joseph was chosen as one out of twelve brothers, and David was preferred as one of his eight brothers. Ester was chosen as one out of hundreds of contestants and Job was favored one of thousands.

A person can appear most unlikely to succeed in the eyes of man but most likely to succeed from God's standpoint. God speaking to the Israelites, *"I did not choose you because you were the greatest, but you were the fewest of all."* And to the Ephesians the Apostle Paul wrote, *"For by grace are you saved, not by works, for it is the grace of God."* Rejoice that God's favor rests upon your life! You are a member of the "chosen" generation.

Ephesians 2:5-8
⁵Even when we were dead in sins, hath quickened us together with Christ, (by grace ye are saved;) ⁶And hath raised us up together, and made us sit together in heavenly places in Christ Jesus: ⁷That in the ages to come he might shew the exceeding riches of his grace in his kindness toward us through Christ Jesus. ⁸For by grace are ye saved through faith; and that not of yourselves: it is the gift of God:

Receiving God's Approval

Most every person who believes in God and His sovereignty has a desire to be approved and pleasing to Him. His Word offers many acts of commission and probably as many acts of omission. He has given the key to all the commandments which simply admonishes us to "study (the Word, the Bible) to show yourself approved by God, *a workman that needs not be ashamed, rightly dividing the word of truth.*"

When you are faithful in this area it will be reflected in your behavior. *"Men will see you good works and glorify your Father in heaven."*

> **2 Timothy 2:15**
>
> [15]Study to shew thyself approved unto God, a workman that needeth not to be ashamed, rightly dividing the word of truth.

God Sees the Really Small Particles

Small articles, items, people, places and things. The minute and even infinite microscopic particles that the strongest microscopes can pick up, God has them already in view.

"Though thy beginning was small, thou latter end shall greatly increase." Perhaps you are greatly concerned about your progress in life or maybe a project that hasn't taken off as you planned. It may seem useless to continue. That is the encouragement given in the Scripture from Job. It's small today but it will increase. You must demonstrate consistent and persistent patience. If you do not become faint, or become disgusted and stop, you will receive the increase.

Things that are small in our eyes, in darkness to the human vision, are magnified and clearly seen by God. As you read this, God saw and willed this scene before your father received the seed that was implanted in your mother's womb.

You, your plans and purposeful struggles were a part of His design for your life. Moses' life began with struggles but his latter end is unmatched even in today's world. The ultimate purpose for Moses and for us is for God's glory to be revealed in our lives.

Job 8:7
⁷*Though thy beginning was small, yet thy latter end should greatly increase.*

Job 42:12
¹²*So the LORD blessed the latter end of Job more than his beginning: for he had fourteen thousand sheep, and six thousand camels, and a thousand yoke of oxen, and a thousand she asses.*

CHAPTER TWELVE

Eternity is For Everyone

Ready in a Moment's Notice

Paul Revere had a plan for emergency warfare defense for the American Colonies in the war with the British. It necessitated a state of readiness for the colonists which required the constant updating of their gear. Even the clothing, boots, cap and coat were to be always ready so they would be able to ride out with a minute's warning. They were called the Minute Men. Their goal was to be ready to defend their homes, families and country whenever the code words were heard, "the British are coming, the British are coming!"

Another example of readiness is seen when teaching a child to read. The student has to be prepared to say (sound) the alphabets, recognize and learn to shape and write the alphabets. Each step is preparing the student for the reading readiness stage. If one of these basic stages are omitted or skipped the student may not progress at the anticipated level.

In John, we are told to remain in a state of readiness because the return of Jesus is not timed nor dated, but always expected. "You do not know the day nor the hour, when the Son of Man shall return." Therefore, we should go to bed, arise and go about our daily schedules, but always ready with a clean slate for the Savior's return. The British are not our concern. Our concern is Jesus' return. Jesus is coming! Jesus is coming!

For the person that is not living in a state of readiness, the Second Return of Jesus will be a big surprise. It will also be too late for the person who is not prepared to face the Lord. We must remember that He keeps every promise, and He has promised that He is coming back in an hour that you think not. **Jesus is coming!**

Matthew 24:29-31

²⁹*Immediately after the tribulation of those days shall the sun be darkened, and the moon shall not give her light, and the stars shall fall from heaven, and the powers of the heavens shall be shaken:* ³⁰*And then shall appear the sign of the Son of man in heaven: and then shall all the tribes of the earth mourn, and they shall see the Son of man coming in the clouds of heaven with power and great glory.* ³¹*And he shall send his angels with a great sound of a trumpet, and they shall gather together his elect from the four winds, from one end of heaven to the other.*

Matthew 24:41, 46

⁴¹*Two women shall be grinding at the mill; the one shall be taken, and the other left.* ⁴⁶*Blessed is that servant, whom his lord when he cometh shall find so doing.*

Show Me The Way To Go Home

There is a song that depicts a fellow who has been away from home on a wild streak of singing, wining and dining. He has money to burn, friends all around and every need imaginable seems fully met.

The fellow in this story is much like the one in the song. He sits in his penthouse where he is finally alone, exhausted from the fun and partying. His nights and weekends are spinning out of control. But they all end the same way: he's tired, frustrated, drained and unfulfilled. There is a longing inside him that he cannot define. For whatever reason money has not been able to secure fulfillment for him. He's beginning to feel that money cannot buy the need that he is seeking.

He experienced excitement with his big time friends and traveling to glamorous places. He even visited one of his city's mega churches. As he reminisced of his world travels, fancy surrounding, famous friends and entertainment, he thought of a little known place. It was the place called home. It wasn't so much the site or the physical location that he was looking for, as it was the memory of the things and people that he had left long ago. These were the people who taught him about God, and he desperately needed someone to show him the way to go home. Airplanes do not land there. He did not need a chauffeur or even MapQuest.

What he came to realize was that he needed, not to return to the physical home site, but rather somebody to show him the way to come to the Christ he learned about when he was young. You could be that person he's searching for. That person could be within a few feet of you every day—on the bus, one the job, in the barbershop, in the check-out line. It could be the repair technician or the person could be in the doctor's office or even the church.

In the Gospel of Luke, there is a very similar story of another young man in a situation much like this fellow in the song.

He may have begged someone to show him the way to go home, not the physical route home, but he longed to get back into the relationship that he once enjoyed. He didn't know how to handle the issue because of how he left home. His immaturity, his attitude of entitlement, the gross lack of respect for his father, family and his disregard for the rules of society regarding inheritance laws made him feel ashamed. It is true, "one can always go home when you can't go anyplace else." But it's good to leave home the way you desire to return. It does not matter what the circumstances were when you left, you are still a family member. Always remember Jesus is waiting for you. Come now, just as you are!

Luke 15:11-32

[11]And he said, A certain man had two sons: [12]And the younger of them said to his father, Father, give me the portion of goods that falleth to me. And he divided unto them his living. [13]And not many days after the younger son gathered all together, and took his journey into a far country, and there wasted his substance with riotous living. [14]And when he had spent all, there arose a mighty famine in that land; and he began to be in want. [15]And he went and joined himself to a citizen of that country; and he sent him into his fields to feed swine. [16]And he would fain have filled his belly with the husks that the swine did eat: and no man gave unto him. [17]And when he came to himself, he said, How many hired servants of my father's have bread enough and to spare, and I perish with hunger! [18]I will arise and go to my father, and will say unto him, Father, I have sinned against heaven, and before thee, [19]And am no more worthy to be called thy son: make me as one of thy hired servants. [20]And he arose, and came to his father. But when he was yet a great way off, his father saw him, and had compassion, and ran, and fell on his neck, and kissed him. [21]And the son said unto him, Father, I have sinned against heaven, and in thy sight, and am no more worthy to be called thy son. [22]But the father said to his servants, Bring forth the best robe, and put it on him; and put a ring on his hand, and shoes on his feet: [23]And bring hither the fatted calf, and kill it; and let us eat, and be merry: [24]For this my son was dead, and is alive again; he was lost, and is found. And they began to be merry.

Is My Life A Clear Reproduction of Christ?

A young man made plans to come to America to visit cousins whom he had never seen. His cousins realized they would not be able to recognize him so they sent him a letter asking him to take a picture of himself and send it to them. They would use the photo to look for him among the hundreds of people coming off the gang plank.

The world does not have a physical picture of Jesus, but seeing a Christian should give them a very accurate picture of what Christ is like, what they can expect to see; not physically but emotionally, spiritually in the overall makeup of the individual—male or female. Christ's attributes would be evident in the person's behavior, devotions, relations, work ethics and entire lifestyle. The question the world is asking: Is that the way Christ would react as they observe our everyday lifestyle?

> **1 Timothy 4:12**
> *12Let no man despise thy youth; but be thou an example of the believers, in word, in conversation, in charity, in spirit, in faith, in purity.*

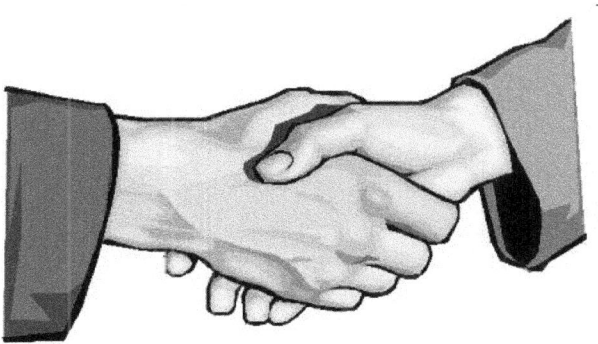

The Old – Unappreciated and Discarded

Many times in our consumer culture we take things for granted.

- Furniture
- Worship music
- Great books
- Beautiful songs
- Poetry
- Jewels
- Property
- Fashionable clothing
- And people!

This list could go on and on but the only thing in the list that has everlasting value is people. The aged are to be revered, respected, honored and even cherished simply because of their age. Eastern cultures are taught to revere the elderly regardless of their station in life. Their wisdom, knowledge and ability to survive commands the respect of the young. The hoary head is a crown of glory, if it be found in the way of righteousness. Proverbs 16:31

> *Leviticus 19:32*
> 32*Thou shalt rise up before the hoary head, and honour the face of the old man. and fear thy God: I am the LORD.*
>
> **Proverbs 16:31**
> 31*The hoary head is a crown of glory, if it be found in the way of righteousness.*

Sowing Seeds

The farmer looks into a container of dry seeds. Some were imperfect, some beginning to rot and some were showing signs of worm infestation. Of course, some were perfectly sound. Anticipating his new crop, he will not plant all of those seeds. He will go through the entire pail and select the very best seeds, and throw away the imperfect seeds.

In our human understanding we select the best seed to be reproduced because we want the very best return on our seeds that are sown. God's Word promises that the seed sown is the exact seed reproduced. The proportions will be multiplied many times over.

The same principle operates with our sharing gifts with others and with God. Some people have been known to share one of their personal cars, clothing, food, finance, etc., only to receive a new automobile, more upscale clothing, multiplied finances, food, etc. God is not concerned with the condition of the money, whether the bills are new, used, moth eaten or wrinkled. His concern is that you realize a good seed for you is a gift representative of what He has blessed you to afford.

Are we giving out of the abundance He has blessed us with, or is our giving a gift simply to say that *"I have given?"* Is He blessed by the example you are setting? It's not the quality of the paper the check is written on or the appearance of the bills, but God observes your faith and the level of your sacrifice.

> ### 2 Corinthians 8:15
> *15As it is written, He that had gathered much had nothing over; and he that had gathered little had no lack.*
> ### Acts 20:35
> *35I have shewed you all things, how that so labouring ye ought to support the weak, and to remember the words of the Lord Jesus, how he said, It is more blessed to give than to receive.*
> ### Luke 6:38
> *38Give, and it shall be given unto you; good measure, pressed down, and shaken together, and running over, shall men give into your bosom. For with the same measure that ye mete withal it shall be measured to you again.*

Many Books...But Only One Book of the Righteous

On a recent trip we passed a long stretch of elaborate homes of palatial designs. The huge gates were closed, from a distance of about a quarter of a mile from the highway, the homes were well kept, the stately doors, and blinds showed no signs of life situated on the sprawling manicured lawns with long tree lined drives. There were no visible signs of children's toys or parked cars.

These are the homes many people dream of owning. It occurred to me that these homes have every available advertised and privately designed protection devices to prevent all unwanted human beings, animals or intruders' entry. However, there exist some unwanted visitors who will find a point of entry. In time the busy little ant and the spider whose web can be found in the stateliest palaces. Insecticides can eliminate them temporarily, but they can often be found in another area of the same building.

There are other undesirables or unwanted guests that can appear and mankind has not found a deterrent for them. They are not restricted to race, creed, color or financial status. These intruders appear in the forms of sickness, age deterioration and death. These invaders enter every home with the birth of every new born baby. These intruders appear in the forms of sickness, age, deterioration and death.

Each new born is entered on a list that is not kept on earth, therefore no one can add to or subtracted from it. All of the world's census records cannot be compared with this heavenly account. As long as babies are born the list continues and no one is eliminated. There is Good News!

The good news is, the space between birth and death and the accompanied unwelcomed guests in life, God is compiling some books of those who lived unrighteous lives (between birth and death and did not repent) they will be listed on the books however, there is only one book for those who lived righteous lives and repented for unrighteousness (between birth and death) while on earth. Since the predestined date of death is uncertain, and if you are not sure of your relationship with the Lord, this is your hour of repentance. To be unlisted in the one and only book of the righteous is to miss heaven eternally.

> ***Revelation 20:12***
> [12] *And I saw the dead, small and great, stand before God; and the books were opened: and another book was opened, which is the book of life: and the dead were judged out of those things which were written in the books, according to their works.*
>
> ***Revelation 21:27***
> *And there shall in no wise enter into it any things that defileth, neither whatsoever worked abomination, or maketh a lie: but they which are written in the Lamb's book of life.*

Jesus is the Center of My Life

This is a beautiful expression that suggests that your life revolves around the Lord. The connection to Him will not permit any actions, thoughts or behaviors that are not consistent with His character. If there are any thoughts, actions, motives or behaviors that are not representative of Christ, it becomes necessary to pray, that your life will exemplify the life of Christ.

> **Philippians 2:5**
> ⁵Let this mind be in you, which was also in Christ Jesus:
> **Philippians 4:2**
> ²I beseech Euodias, and beseech Syntyche, that they be of the same mind in the Lord.

CHAPTER THIRTEEN

Discipleship

Staying on the Outskirts

When a beast of prey sees a herd of grazing animals, the predator will stake out one in the herd that appears easiest to attack with the least effort. Usually these are the youngest and almost always those that are in the rear and on the outer edges of the pack. Those that are in the front and in the inner circle receive the greatest protection, because of their location in the herd. Those on the outer edge and outskirts are in the greatest danger for attack.

Individuals who come to Christ must be careful not to follow Him on the outskirts. Following Christ on the outskirts is equivalent to slothful church attendance, lax participation, irregular personal devotions and Bible study.

Following on the outskirts also includes refusal to accept a responsibility or an assignment in church ministry. All of these place the child of God in direct range for enemy attack. When following close up, near the center or in the front, the probability of an attack is much less because of the group's surrounding support of prayers and Bible teachings.

> ### Hebrews 6:11-12
> [11]And we desire that every one of you do shew the same diligence to the full assurance of hope unto the end: [12]That ye be not slothful, but followers of them who through faith and patience inherit the promises.
>
> ### 2 Timothy 2:15-16
> [15] Study to shew thyself approved unto God, a workman that needeth not to be ashamed, rightly dividing the word of truth. [16]But shun profane and vain babblings: for they will increase unto more ungodliness.
>
> ### 2 Timothy 2:22
> [22]Flee also youthful lusts: but follow righteousness, faith, charity, peace, with them that call on the Lord out of a pure heart.
>
> ### 2 Timothy 2:26
> [26]And that they may recover themselves out of the snare of the devil, who are taken captive by him at his will.
>
> ### Hebrews 12:14
> [14]Follow peace with all men, and holiness, without which no man shall see the Lord.

The World's Largest Turnaround

As individuals of African American heritage, our foreparents were enslaved, in bondage with no personal property, legal rights, not even their biological children were considered their own. The slave masters frequently sold the slave children for the best price while the parents looked on sadly with tears and heart rending pleas. Ignored and not given one cent from the sale of their flesh and blood. All their worldly goods could have easily been stored in a flour sack. They did not in their ability to acquire possessions or wealth, nor did they trust in the arm of flesh. Their survival depended entirely on the love and grace of God.

Herein lies the world's greatest turnaround. Just a few generations forward, we have acquired a measure of liberty, properties, even some leisure boats, airplanes, etc. However, our children or their offspring have rewritten the use of the days on the calendar. Sunday is no longer the day of worship but car washing, mowing lawns, boats in tow on the way to the lakes, and shopping mall parking lots are overrun. Monday Nite Football and other sports are no longer associated with one night of the week. Any night of the week and all day Saturdays and Sundays beginning late mornings until the ten o'clock news hour the radio and television programs are dominated by sports.

We're losing our sense of thankfulness and our sense of responsibility. On a larger scale, we have failed to pass on a sense of responsibility of honoring God. Future generations will not have a full knowledge of God's wonderful works of grace He has bestowed upon us. It is quite apparent that neither by word nor example are we the witnesses to God's love, grace, gifts, salvation and miraculous provisions to us. God would have us to say thanks and show our thankfulness by the way we teach our children.

Deuteronomy 11:18-21

[18]Therefore shall ye lay up these my words in your heart and in your soul, and bind them for a sign upon your hand, that they may be as frontlets between your eyes. [19]And ye shall teach them your children, speaking of them when thou sittest in thine house, and when thou walkest by the way, when thou liest down, and when thou risest up. [20]And thou shalt write them upon the door posts of thine house, and upon thy gates: [21]That your days may be multiplied, and the days of your children, in the land which the LORD sware unto your fathers to give them, as the days of heaven upon the earth.

Proverbs 22:6

[6]Train up a child in the way he should go: and when he is old, he will not depart from it.

Prayer Really is Effective

"Man ought to always pray and not faint," is frequently stated when someone is faced with a difficult situation. The prayer is indeed the precursor to the answer to any problem but the prayer of faith must be mixed with constancy. The last three words of the sentence is "and not faint" which means not to grow tired, disheartened, discouraged and give up the effort.

If there's an outbreak of a deadly disease, each person exposed to the virus may not die. Some may have full blown symptoms yet recover while others may exhibit only a few of the symptoms and not recover. The difference is in the body's pre-conditioned ability (its immune system) to resist viral attacks.

In the body of Christ, when one is facing an enemy attack, the level of strength of the individual or the church to withstand and forcefully resist the enemy to a large extent depends on the prayerful persistence of those involved. When one is aware of an enemy's approach that individual will be stronger if they have prayed and continue in prayer.

Praying preconditions the individual to resist the adversary's deadly blows. A physically weak immune system in the human body cannot resist a deadly viral attack resulting in death, however, with proper medical care the immune system can be built up and reverse or reduce the impact of the virus.

One may ask, "If the blows are *this* powerful and the situation is *this* bad and I *am* praying, what might the outcome be if I neglect to seek God in prayer? The prayers of the righteous avails (accomplishes) much and without prayer some desires may not be realized.

Luke 18:1-7

¹And he spake a parable unto them to this end, that men ought always to pray, and not to faint; ²Saying, There was in a city a judge, which feared not God, neither regarded man: ³And there was a widow in that city; and she came unto him, saying, Avenge me of mine adversary. ⁴And he would not for a while: but afterward he said within himself, Though I fear not God, nor regard man; ⁵Yet because this widow troubleth me, I will avenge her, lest by her continual coming she weary me. ⁶And the Lord said, Hear what the unjust judge saith. ⁷And shall not God avenge his own elect, which cry day and night unto him, though he bear long with them?

Sleeping is a Dangerous Time

The story is told of a hunter who gradually lost his way in the forest. Realizing he was lost and darkness was falling fast, he was unable to make contact with any of his fellow hunters. Fearful he realized his only recourse was to gather some wood, encircle himself in a large circle and light the fires to protect himself and provide warmth though the cold winter night. Inside the circle he had plenty of firewood. As the fire blazed he felt very comfortable knowing that the heat and the blaze would keep the animals away.

As the night wore on, he felt so cozy and comfortable he

began dozing and without realizing it he was sound asleep. Suddenly, he was awakened and alert and could clearly see all around pairs of eyes focused entirely on him. Frightened and seeing his dilemma as the brightly burning fire had died down to a circle of burned out embers, he understood he had fallen asleep in a dangerous time.

The lost man found himself in a predicament because he failed to keep the hot fire stirred and refueled. The result was the fire he had enjoyed began settling and was dying out to the cold winds of the night.

Our walk with God is strengthened through our consistent studies in the Bible, prayer and faithful assembling with others in worship and service. Without persistence in these areas, our walk with God, much like the comforting warm fire, will be abated and eventually die out. We will lose our passion for the things of the Spirit. Our walk with God can be likened to the lost traveler falling asleep surrounded by the comfort of the coziest blazes. It will return to its former cold and lifeless state.

1 Timothy 4:13
13Till I come, give attendance to reading, to exhortation, to doctrine.

Hebrews 10:25
25Not forsaking the assembling of ourselves together, as the manner of some is; but exhorting one another: and so much the more, as ye see the day approaching.

Hebrews 11:6
6But without faith it is impossible to please him: for he that cometh to God must believe that he is, and that he is a rewarder of them that diligently seek him.

Hebrews 12:11
11Now no chastening for the present seemeth to be joyous, but grievous: nevertheless afterward it yieldeth the peaceable fruit of righteousness unto them which are exercised thereby.

First Things First

Through your own efforts, it has been impossible to enjoy a debt free lifestyle. When God becomes your business manager, worry-free living is only one of the benefits that accompany the money management plan outlined in Scripture. The world has not experienced the many ways that God will arrange for those who will make His plan #1. Some who have received debt cancellations, rebates, special discounts, bonuses, one of a kind specials, etc., are among those persons who faithfully follow God's pre-arranged plan for financial success. Implementing the plan backed up by the Lord assures you that you will profit legitimately because "the *riches of the Lord addeth no sorrow to it."* Here's the Lord's financial plan:

Number One

- Seek ye first, the kingdom of God and His righteousness (diligently search until you find, and become involved in the kingdom things that pertain to God and His righteous way of living and the managing of your business affairs).

- And all these things (including things that money cannot buy) will be added unto you. Many things that money cannot purchase such as good health, Divine protection and family welfare are added benefits of God's financial plan.

> *Malachi 3:7-11*
> *[7]Even from the days of your fathers ye are gone away from mine ordinances, and have not kept them. Return unto me, and I will return unto you, saith the LORD of hosts. But ye said, Wherein shall we return? [8]Will a man rob God? Yet ye have robbed me. But ye say, Wherein have we robbed thee? In tithes and offerings. [9]Ye are cursed with a curse: for ye have robbed me, even this whole nation. [10]Bring ye all the tithes into the storehouse, that there may be meat in mine house, and prove me now herewith, saith the LORD of hosts, if I will not open you the windows of heaven, and pour you out a blessing, that there shall not be room enough to receive it. [11]And I will rebuke the devourer for your sakes, and he shall not destroy the fruits of your ground; neither shall your vine cast her fruit before the time in the field, saith the LORD of hosts.*

Children at Play

In 1 Peter 3:12 the Bible says that *"The eyes of the Lord are over the righteous, and his ears are open unto their prayer."* The righteous have two promises in this verse that are not available to the ungodly. The first assurance is that they are never out of His sight. The driver of an automobile frequently encounters a "blind side" on the road, but with God there is never a blind side. He assures the righteous that His eyes are encircling them.

When looking over an object you can see it from all angles. So we can never be out of sight to Him. The Psalmist says, *"If I ascend to the heavens, thou are there or if I make my bed in hell, thou are there."* Night and day is the same to God.

The second assurance of the righteous is that we can always have an audience with Him. The promise that His ears are open to our prayers conveys the idea of our God who is ready, waiting and has entirely attentive ears for our prayers.

Perhaps you can recall times during your early childhood, when you were outside with friends and the eyes of your mother watched for your safety from the window or doorway. It may have appeared that you were out at play alone but it is a fact that she constantly kept you under her watch. So is the watchful care of God and His attentiveness to our prayers which are multiplied many times greater than that of our earthly parents. You may find yourself in some very tragic, precarious and awkward situations, but do not become alarmed. He is focused on your location and His ears are tuned to hear your prayer today. God does not get our names confused nor even our voice tones. We can be assured *He knows them that are His* and He knows every one's name.

2 Peter 2:9
⁹The Lord knoweth how to deliver the godly out of temptations, and to reserve the unjust unto the day of judgment to be punished:

2 Timothy 4:18
¹⁸And the Lord shall deliver me from every evil work, and will preserve me unto his heavenly kingdom: to whom be glory for ever and ever. Amen.

2 Thessalonians 3:3
³But the Lord is faithful, who shall stablish you, and keep you from evil.

2 Timothy 2:19
¹⁹Nevertheless the foundation of God standeth sure, having this seal, The Lord knoweth them that are his. And, let every one that nameth the name of Christ depart from iniquity.

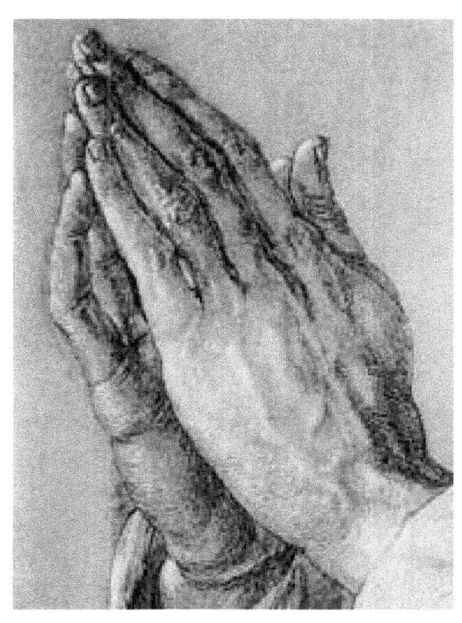

Affirmations From A-Z

A   I am anointed and my steps are ordered by God. 2 Cor. 1:21

B   I am blessed, God says so. Psalms 128: 1

C   I am a child of the King of Kings. 1 John 3:2

D   I am divinely appointed and destined to win. Joshua 1:7-8

E   I will excel, no evil shall befall me. Romans 8:31

F   Failures may occur, but I will not be unfruitful. Psalms 1:3

G   God is my source. Proverbs 15:6

H   I will endeavor to bring Honor to His name. Joshua 8: 49; Malachi 1:6

I   I will fear no evil, for the Lord is with me. Psalms 23:4

J   Jesus is the first, last and all in between. Isaiah 44:6b

K   I am kept by the blood of Jesus. Hebrews 9:14; 1 John 1:7

L   The love of Jesus will never fail me. Jeremiah 31:3; Deut. 23:5

M   I have a new mind, the mind-set of Christ. Philippians 2:5

N	I have not the spirit of fear, but of faith and power. Isaiah 41:10
O	I will use every opportunity to show the world Christ. Is. 40:9-10
P	In Him I am protected, productive and powerful. Phil. 4: 13
Q	I will study to be quiet and attend to my affairs. Isaiah 30:15
R	I will not rest until my family is in the arc of safety. Matt. 10: 32-33
S	Come what may, I am committed to serve God. 2 Cor. 6:16-17
T	In everything I will give thanks. 1 Thessalonians 5: 18
U	Unexplained, misunderstood, I remain unchanged.1 Cor. 15: 58
V	With Jesus I shall not be the victim, but the victor. I Cor. 15: 57
W	I will keep the mind-set that, "All Is Well." Psalms 128:2
X	Jesus died for all even the unnamed 'X' generation. John 3: 16
Y	I will yield my entire body to serve the Lord. Romans 6: 12-13
Z	If only one word, with zeal, I'll say it for Jesus. Num. 25: 11-13

About the Author

Pearl Cooper White, a native of Mobile, Alabama, resides in Shreveport, Louisiana. A Southern University graduate, she is a retired Secondary Counselor, a National Board Certified Counselor (NBCC), adjunct professor of Psychology at LSU, and a life member of Alpha Kappa Alpha.

Her local church ministry includes Sanctuary Prayer Leader, the Marriage Ministry Coordinator and the Allendale District Missionary.

Opportunities for mission work have taken her to Africa (Malawi; Nairobi, Kenya) and to Haitian area townships. For eighteen years she was the Department of Women's Jurisdictional Secretary and served in the National Department of Women as the Aspiring Missionary's instructor.

Missionary White is married to the former principal, Lt. Colonel (Ret) Walter N. White. They have three children: Mrs. Tania White Jackson, MD and husband Gary (Frisco, TX); Ms. Kristi C. White (Atlanta, GA); and Elder Walter White, Jr. and wife Shronda (Wiley, TX). They are blessed with six grandchildren.

Copies of this book are available by contacting Mrs. Pearl C. White at paseokidz@aol.com.

www.ingramcontent.com/pod-product-compliance
Lightning Source LLC
Chambersburg PA
CBHW061946070426
42450CB00007BA/1065